The Engineer's Daughter

M.V. Williams

PublishAmerica
Baltimore

© 2004 by M.V. Williams.
All rights reserved. No part of this book may be reproduced, stored in a retrieval system or transmitted in any form or by any means without the prior written permission of the publishers, except by a reviewer who may quote brief passages in a review to be printed in a newspaper, magazine or journal.

First printing

ISBN: 1-4137-4962-3
PUBLISHED BY PUBLISHAMERICA, LLLP
www.publishamerica.com
Baltimore

Printed in the United States of America

This book is dedicated to all those who struggle to leave their families, and to my own husband and children who provided my escape route and have remained a constant source of encouragement and love.

M.V. Williams lives with her husband in a small cottage in a forgotten corner of England. Having been a mother, teacher, trader, psychotherapist and poet, she now writes at home, grows vegetables and paints. She has published several self-help books, poetry and stories.

The Engineer's Daughter

ONE

I left home for the second time at the age of forty-seven. It was five o'clock on a freezing Sunday morning in January and nobody was about. My mother, who always rose early, was dead. The funeral had been in October; now it was New Year and a terrible madness had settled upon the family. My father snored upstairs in the stuffy bedroom they had shared until her last illness, bitter, angry, and exhausted. My brother was, I imagined, locked in his bedroom as he always was, listening to the sounds of his house in the darkness on the edge of sleep, vigilant; still waiting for my mother's call. I warmed my hands on the Aga and rooted around for a biro in the kitchen drawer. I left a note for my brother telling him that I wasn't staying where I wasn't welcome and to please give back the things my mother had left me in her will. Then I stepped out into the icy darkness. I pushed the key carefully through the letterbox so that it just rested inside the flap without falling. I didn't want it to fall with a clang on the kitchen tiles; someone might have woken and although I knew they wouldn't come after me, I wanted them to understand that I was already far away. Long gone.

So, I was on the outside now, and my heart was beating fast.

Around me was a total, soft, dense, familiar blackness, unbroken by any glimmer of light. The house was up a long drive bordered by overhanging trees and there were no streetlights in the lane. There were no neighbours. I wasn't frightened; all the frightening things were back in the house I had just left. The madness of grief, my brother's anger that my mother had deserted him and left him in charge of my father, the crazy finances, my sister's hatred; these I was glad to be leaving. The sun would not be up for more than two hours. Ice glittered on the driveway in spangles; stars glittered above. I felt exhilarated and free. Down the dark road I walked, blood racing through my veins, to the station two miles away and the London train. I had my own home, my own family. Reclaiming them would help me put the past where it belonged, back in the house I had just left. Self-willed, mulish, I had escaped before, many years ago, and there was no going back.

Then, I was seventeen; not beautiful, but photos show a certain something that attracted male admirers, though I was still a virgin. I was a stroppy, opinionated girl, who did not treat men with the reverence my mother thought seemly, though she was hardly a good example, as she hated my father and took her frustrations out on me, letting me know how worthless she felt he was. I was supposed to side with her but somehow I couldn't. Really, I just wanted her to sort it all out with him and leave me alone to get on with my life. I had fallen in love.

My boyfriend, Charles, had a motorbike and a leather jacket—I'm not sure which impressed me more—and wanted me to go with him to Eel-Pie Island. My mother was dead set against the idea; my father was indifferent. He reasoned that if I was old enough to go to work, I was old enough to decide how to spend my leisure time, and my mother was furious with him for not backing her. I remember what I was wearing that night—skin-tight jeans and a black rollneck sweater. I don't remember the shoes; I preferred going barefoot then. It was orthodox clothing, but my mother complained bitterly about the jeans. I had rings of kohl around my eyes, and black mascara. My hair was plaited in a single braid, which fell over my left shoulder.

After a bitter row, I escaped from the house. She wouldn't give me a key and told me that if I came back late, I would be locked out. This was the ultimate sanction and one I had never dared to break. I thought about this. It was a warm midsummer evening, and there was a wild, restless magic in the air. I was in love. I could live with being locked out. Sensing trouble when he came, Charles did not go into the house. Instead, he turned the bike around and I climbed on, my long plait tucked inside my jacket, arms wrapped around his broad chest, comfortingly. And we left. It seemed so unbelievably simple, so straightforward an action after all the rows and recriminations.

Oh the exhilaration of that summer night! Flying along the country lanes, bending and rolling, sweeping round corners, weaving through potholes, all the way up to London.

I pictured my mother in the kitchen with the words she'd never say to me now: *Be Careful, Don't Let Him Take Advantage of You, Don't Let Anyone Put Something in Your Drink, Arab Men Will Make You Their White Slave, The Best Contraceptive Is the Little Word No, Men Won't Respect You If,* and *You Think You Know It All* (true).

The things I would like to have heard her say were *Have a Good Time, How Exciting! I Trust You to Use Your Common Sense, I'll Leave a Key Out, You Look Great* and *Tell Charles I'm Trusting Him to Look After You*. But trust was something my mother didn't have; too many bad things had happened to her and she would never trust anyone until the day she died, especially men.

She must have known we'd gone anyway, and when we zoomed back in the wee small hours, elated with the night, each other and the espresso coffee drunk in the all night Cafe Macabre, to find the door locked and the key missing from its usual place on the lilac tree, we took the coats from the porch and spread them under the trees at the end of the garden and slept together there. Although I crept in the next morning while my mother was in the washhouse, I didn't fool her for a moment and she let me have the full force of her contempt and fury. But by then it was too late, my ears were blocked with freedom and my eyes had seen the bright lights of the Holy City and there was no turning back. Shortly after I turned eighteen, I left home.

Over the years I hoped to gain her approval and her trust, but despite a career, a marriage and three children and nothing going disastrously wrong with any of them, approval was slow to come and the negative view of the world prevailed.

Don't You Think You Should, and *What on Earth Do You Want to,* and *You'll Never* became watchwords, stabbing and accusing. I kept my distance; attacks could be dealt with better if I had the bodyguard of my family around me. See, somebody likes me, even if you don't. And they didn't. I had freedom and didn't have to put up with what they endured, so often disguised as love, with *I'm Only Concerned for Your Happiness* and *You Children Are All I've Got,* and *I'm Just Trying to Give*

You Some Advice, and, most insidious of all, *What Would I Do Without You?* There were warning messages about *Out There*, and a degree of paranoia, with *They All*, and *You Can't Trust Them* and *They're All The Same*.

I told my husband after a particularly difficult visit: "I feel I'm all alone," and he sensibly replied, "You've got us—they're the ones that are alone." And it was true, and I recognised it eagerly and knew why I'd married this man. And the friendly, concerned faces of my children told me it was their truth too. Neither of my siblings made the journey to freedom after me; too afraid of *Out There* to flee the nest, too confused to understand why they were prisoners, their dreary years of waiting ending only when my mother died and a new sort of waiting began. The words of William Blake rang in my ears: *"For the time of youth had fled/And grey hairs were on my head."* Never now would they have their own partners or children. Bitter and bereft, they clung to the nest breaking up beneath them, snatching at anything to protect them from the abyss below.

Now they became my accusers and *You Weren't Here* and *You Don't Know* and *Why Are You Doing This* and *She Would Have Wanted* became the cries. Unable to communicate, and unwilling to face the real loss of their adulthood, their bitterness became palpable. My father, full of regrets and his own sorrow, withdrew into his own private world. Always his habitual retreat when life was not paying him attention, he vanished more and more into the prison of his past.

So it was that once again, at the age of forty-seven, I stepped through the front door of what had once been my childhood home and knew that I had left it for a second time, and this time it was for good.

The intervening years shift and change in my memory like the patterns in a kaleidoscope. There had been many separations, not of my choosing, when my mother had been ill, and we too young to protest. The world after the War was still fragmented and my father, who was working hard and studying at night school, felt unable to look after us. Neighbours and aunts filled in where they could, until we reached school age. Boarding school had been a part of both my parents' childhood experience. Suddenly, when I was six, it was to become mine.

TWO

We had been to school before, briefly; to a Peterborough infant school, where I learned little that was of any use to me, except that I did not enjoy being made to take an afternoon nap on a rolled up mat on the floor of the large hall with the other reception class infants. I adored my teacher, whom I immediately christened Miss Prancer, though I have an idea her real name was something similar, and who was tall, pretty, and wore wide, floaty skirts that twirled around her as she moved above us napping infants on the floor. Sometimes, for a treat, we were allowed to spread newspaper out on the floor, put sheets of sugar paper out on it, and paint. Miss Prancer was a brave woman, not seeming to mind too much about the water pots knocked over by eager little infants. I left this Paradise all too soon and went up into the first class, ruled by a Mrs. Pritchard, who wore lavender tweed suits and had steel grey hair twisted into metallic rolls at the base of her neck. Mrs. Pritchard ruled with a rod of iron; her classroom was silent, and rows of watchful frightened faces tried vainly to anticipate whom she would pick on next.

Ouch! The boy sitting next to me jabbed at my arm with his inky metal pen-nib and drew blood, and the shock of the attack made me gasp and then yell out in outrage, but despite the inky, bloody mark on my arm, I do not remember him being punished, and it seemed as if I were held to blame for not keeping quiet about this assault. The highlight of the day was milk time, when the small bottles, which had been lined up around the tortoise stove in the corner to warm them, were given out by the milk monitors, who placed in each one a flabby waxed paper straw. Children were often hungry then, and we had no allotment like other families in the street to provide us with extras. Every street had its smelly bin for pig feed in those early postwar years, and the one in our street smelled sourly of potato peelings and cabbage stalks. It was my job to put our scraps in this bin. I felt shocked when I found there were papers from someone's fish dinner in there, but for some reason my parents thought it amusing. Miss Pritchard's class did not improve. I hated school and began to be ill and had a great deal of time off school with asthma and tonsillitis, and then was bullied in the playground by children amazed that I hadn't yet learned the sequence of *The Big Ship Sails Through the Alley Alley-Oo*, nor did I know the words of *Put Another Nickel in, In the Nickel Odeon*. It seems I sang it all wrong, and the big girls made me sing my version over and over so that they could laugh at me. My asthma got worse and the Peterborough air didn't improve it, laden as it was with the fumes from the sugar beet factory and the brewery, and the fog from the fens.

I would wake in the night, feeling an iron band around my chest, as I struggled to breathe. My asthma got worse as my mother became more and more unhappy. Tension and stress in her created desperation in me not to be at school away from her, though she never encouraged this. The spasms in my chest were a response to the tensions I felt. My deaf, vulnerable, unhappy mother—was it safe to leave her? The asthma gripped me so that I was gasping for air, and my very survival felt as though it was threatened. Standing in front of an open window, and steam in the bathroom, seemed to relieve it a little, but with the asthma and the frequent ear infections and tonsillitis I was also experiencing, it is not surprising that I lost almost a year of school. Having my tonsils out helped a little, and by the time we moved back to where my mother felt happier, my health had improved. But in Peterborough, I hated school anyway and the more I missed, the harder it was to get back to where my classmates were up to.

"Caroline!" It's my mother calling me down the garden. "Where are you?"

I go further down behind the bush. The raw stalk of rhubarb I have picked is sour and stringy, but I munch along its scarlet stem with determination. I have been told often enough that eating raw rhubarb will give me a tummy ache, but so far it hasn't worked. I wish, I wish, *I wish*, I could be really ill, so that I don't have to go to school.

"Caroline!" Her voice is getting angry. "It's time for you to go to school."

Janet pipes up and tells my mother where I am hiding. The rhubarb is snatched out of my hand and I am dragged towards the front garden and the neighbour's car and thrust inside, screaming and crying. The neighbour doesn't offer to give us a lift again.

Our mother stayed in a lot and moped. The deafness, which had troubled her as a young woman had returned, and she had made no new friends in Peterborough. Far from her aunt, who had brought her up, and her mother, stricken with rheumatoid arthritis, she pined for her home in Hampshire. Father took to trying his hand at cooking as he felt my mother was incompetent at it. According to him she was incompetent at most things.

Father arrives through the door one Saturday clutching green nets full of peas bought in the market and puts them into the pressure cooker to make pea soup, ignoring my mother's distress at having her domain taken over. It's a disaster. The peas are stringy and he puts too much salt in. We don't like the dirty green colour and refuse to eat it. Later, he tries his hand at Swiss rolls and sponge cake.

"Edith! Oy!" (Because of her deafness, he often shouts this at her). "Come and look at this." There he stands, pleased as punch, demanding my mother admire his handiwork and when the pea soup refuses to pass through the hair sieve and the Swiss roll unrolls and the cake sinks in the middle, he angrily gives up his attempts at cooking, blaming the stove, the ingredients and my mother, and goes back to tinkering with her sewing machine. Nothing he attempts turns out quite right these days, but later he decides to apply his design and engineering skills to making clothes for the family, now that he has fixed the sewing machine. My mother is the recipient of a long, circular patchwork skirt, made of multicoloured seersucker and sewn with great precision. She looks lovely in it, and he is moved to make her another, and us some seersucker sundresses. These are attractive, though we quickly outgrow them. My mother tells us not to tell everyone who made our clothes; it's not a thing men do. My mother has the equivalent of a degree in textile design herself and possesses real talent as a designer and draughtsman, but my father is undermining her very quickly.

"You're doing that all wrong," he says, taking the item away from her.

"You'll never do it like that." And she gives in, not daring to argue with him.

Once he's made something successfully, he moves on to a new challenge, and he rarely repeats his successes. It's as if he wants to show my mother that her underdeveloped skills as a housewife are totally inadequate. *See, I can do what you do, with no trouble at all. It's easy, a worthless skill really.* He cannot bear for her to outdo him in any way. His sole contribution to the cooking for the household after this first attempt is rum butter; to go with the Christmas puddings my mother makes each year.

My parents have a wind up gramophone and at Christmas they play our favourite record, *One Day My Prince Will Come* and *Hi Ho, Hi Ho, It's Off to Work We Go*, while we gaze at the pictures of Snow White and do jerky little dances in time to the music. My father has a large collection of records, mostly Latin American music and some light classics. He tries hard to instil a love of this music in us, taking us to see *The Tales of Hoffman*, which we are far too young to enjoy. As always he finds it hard to enter our world and demands that we enter his. Our mother takes us to see *Bambi* and *Snow White*, knowing we will find it enchanting. Our father resolutely stays at home, thinking it beneath him and not wishing to be part of our entertainment.

Our house is a prewar semi, with a small garden backing onto the showground, now a housing estate. The garden has little of interest in it, except a rhubarb patch and some climbing roses. My sister and I dig away at the end of the garden with our small tin spades, after my father tells us we might reach Australia. We reach sandy soil in our hole and keep digging, certain that we'll come out somewhere else. There is a blackbird's nest behind the shed, perched on the fence; other than that the garden is devoid of any life except for the snails. We pick them up and try to make them race along the path but they refuse to be organised and head back to the water butt the minute our backs are turned. At two and a half, I have a tricycle with yellow wheels. Tired of the garden and its limited attractions, I open the gate and cycle off up the pavement to see what the world around the corner has to offer. My mother comes puffing up alongside.

"Where do you think you're going?"

"Just looking round corner." My little fingers point up the street.

"Well don't do it again, you might get lost." Jerked roughly back into the garden, where the gate was tied, I reflected on my misdemeanour. It was my first lesson in what might happen to me if I ventured away from home. *Lost* was not something we could really understand the implications of. Mothers always found you, it seemed, despite your attempts to leave them. Janet was properly lost for a while at the London Zoo, when my mother took us there. If our father was there with us, I don't remember it. He generally opted out of any family outings unless they were his idea. My frantic mother, hearing aid dangling, dragged me along the paths under the canal until we found my sister watching the monkeys' tea party. The relief on my mother's face let me understand what *lost* meant to her. I, too, had been scared that my loved and hated little sister might have been taken away by nasty men and I would be alone with my parents once again. She seemed unconcerned by the drama she had caused, and I felt warm towards her because she was now the naughty one instead of me. Usually my rebellious, loud and inquisitive nature would mean that I was the one who got into trouble most often, while she looked sweet and shy and avoided censure.

My father did try to be a father to his little daughters at times, and took us out in a double pram to shop in the town, but like most of his attempts to get things right this, too, went wrong. Parking us under the biggest pigeon roost in town was not a good idea, and our mother complained loudly when he brought back the filthy pram. He didn't try again. He watched us from a distance, always, not knowing how to deal with us. He didn't understand our needs, as no one had understood his. He had friends in Peterborough, old friends who tolerated his eccentricities and with whom he had warm trusting relationships. Great Yarmouth, where my mother grew up, was not so far away and we occasionally stayed with my mother's sister who lived there and visited my grandmother.

Now my grandmother, whom I hardly know, is ill. For years she has been crippled with rheumatoid arthritis and she sits in a special chair, her white hair in a bun on top of her head, her face pale and neat, with sharp black eyebrows, cared for by Aggie. Aggie came to live with the family as a girl when she was left homeless after her own parents died. She has looked after her adopted family ever since. My mother is jealous of Aggie, who has stayed with the family while my mother was sent away to live with Aunt Ethel after her father died.

My grandmother was not a young parent. My mother, the fourth child, was born when she was forty and the relationship was not a warm one. But someone somewhere, perhaps her father, treated my mother with love and kindness for the first eight years of her life, or she would not have been a good mother to us. Perhaps my grandmother began to be ill after the birth of my mother, perhaps she had simply run out of the energy to be a loving parent by the time my mother was born.

My grandmother suffers a crisis and is taken into hospital. My mother stays with her, expecting the worst, but the old lady recovers and my mother, reassured, returns to Peterborough. Her mother continues to improve. Then, one morning, she announces, with uncharacteristic firmness, that my father will have to look after us. She has to go to Yarmouth, now, to the hospital. My father argues with her. He does not want to be left with us. There has been no telegram, and the latest news has been positive. What is this panic about, he wants to know. She grabs her bag and leaves. Half an hour later, the telegram messenger arrives on his motorbike, saying he had been unable to find our address. The telegram is brief: COME AT ONCE MOTHER DYING.

This is the first of many occasions when we realise that our mother seems to possess some strange knowledge about things without anyone telling her. Shortly after this we move back to Hampshire and continue our schooling at Wendlesham Hall. My father is not happy with the move. He had lived here in Peterborough before for a few years and been happy. One by one, his friends have settled down and married. He wants to cling on to these friendships, the tennis club, the dance halls, and the sense of belonging he experiences there, but my mother never feels she fits in and makes very little effort to try. He is very upset to leave the town and the security it represents but my mother is homesick and so, after two years, we leave. There is another reason for us leaving, my Great-Aunt Ethel is ill. My mother is about to lose the last older family member who means anything to her. She needs to go back to the one place she thinks of as home.

My father misses his friends and familiar surroundings, but comforts himself by buying a rundown cottage and converting it into a family home for all of us. But this, too, is denied to him. Fate keeps on intervening in our family life. We have not been in our new home long before my mother's aunt dies, leaving the house to my mother. So she returns to her family home, the possessor of it, and my father has to sell the cottage. Nothing now will go right for him. My mother is pregnant again, and he hopes he will have a son. Giving her the children she wants is all he can do to make her happy, it seems. Later, he discovers that his son will inherit the house and my mother will leave him nothing, especially not her love.

THREE

When I was born, my parents lived in a small, rented, thatched cottage, with a well in the courtyard and mice and earwigs in the thatch. Gas lit, unheated, damp, it was my home for the first two years of my life. My mother, pregnant again with my sister when I am not quite a year old, loves this little house with its apple trees and iron pump. My father is, in his words, tickled pink that his new wife should have conceived so quickly and that I should have been born without complications or fuss in the cottage hospital. Despite a bomb landing on the hospital when my mother is bathing me, and the food rationing, there is a spirit of optimism. The D Day landings happen the week after my birth, and the tired soldiers begin to return home in the years that follow. England has to lick her wounds. My mother breastfeeds me, recovers well from the birth and all is well. Active very young, I totter around the garden at nine months old, run at a year. My pants are falling down because there is a shortage of rubber to make effective elastic. My hair is soft at the base of my neck, my skin is smooth and pale and my parents are delighted with me. The faded, pink rayon romper suits or dresses I wear are second or third hand, because material is scarce. One has puffed sleeves and hand-smocking around the bodice, and I am photographed wearing it, with my parents looking pleased behind me. My father is behind my mother and me, looking on.

My father has given my mother a new toy and she's pleased with it, so he's pleased with me. It was what she always wanted, and what he had wanted to give her to make her happy. He was the price she paid for having children. The second pregnancy took my mother's attention away from me, and I made up for the lack by being the apple of my great-aunt's eye. But I missed my mother.

When my mother went into hospital to give birth to my sister, I stayed at Somersets with my great-aunt, while my father came and went, unwelcome as always in this house of women. Despite their care of me, I did not cope well with my mother's absence. There were to be many absences later.

It's cold tonight, with a chill breathy fog on the fields, as our car wends its way up the long winding drive to Wendlesham Hall School. Bundled into our rough tweed coats with the leather buttons and muffled against the cold, we have also been made to wear our liberty bodices under hand knitted jumpers to keep out the freezing fog, but the rubber buttons of the liberty bodices have become cracked and perished with constant washing, so that they keep coming undone. It's a strange sensation, feeling your underwear freeing itself from your body. My sister and I sit in the back, on the leather-smelling upholstery of the family car, a Citroen Light Fifteen, which only my father is able to control. The long drive is very dark; and we peer out hopefully, though the back seat is low and we are small, but only the faint white outline of a hockey goalpost shows up against the darkness of the lawns to the right, and to the left are fields of ploughed earth as far as the eye can see, wreathed in shreds of gauzy dampness. As we drive up the slope to the main building, we pass between two tall, dense, holly trees, on either side of the drive. On this dark night, they seem to have a symbolic presence, gloomy and forbidding, guarding the entrance to this imposing building that looms over acres of rolling parkland at the front, while at the back it dwindles into a collection of ramshackle buildings and outhouses that in turn give way onto the kitchen garden and shrubbery. But we know nothing about these mysteries, only gawp in wonder at what we can see, pillars, marble, brass, window after window.

My mother has been a pupil at the school herself and thinks that we might benefit from the education it offers. I am six and a half, my sister five.

Janet jumps out of the car first, her auburn curls bobbing. I pull her back in my bossy, big sister way, and we accompany our parents up to the front door. So huge! It dwarfs all the doors on our cottage. The bell rings with a loud and mournful echo deep inside the house and after a minute or two a light flickers on. The door creaks open and there she stands, a person so tiny and misshapen that Janet and I stare openmouthed at her. Her starched white maid's cap and apron look incongruent on her twisted little body. Her face has been twisted with palsy, dragging her right eye downward into a red liquid rim. She asks us to come in and wait, then shuffles off along the corridor to fetch the Misses Potts.

"Her name's Maisie," confides my mother, in a loud whisper. "She's quite harmless, poor soul. She was here when I was a girl."

"Oh!" we chorus in wonder. The room we are in is huge, and dark, and the gas lamps are turned down low. I notice something gleaming on the parquet floor. It is the glass eyes of a stuffed tiger's head, the skin stretched out on the floor behind it. I become more interested and have to be restrained from sitting on it. The dry, furry smell tickles my nose and makes me want to sneeze. It is part of the concoction of scent in that room; mothballs, coal gas, and mildew. I want desperately to stuff my fingers into the tiger's mouth and feel the sharpness of those white ivory teeth for myself. My father restrains me as I pull a face.

A grand piano fills the other end of the room, all dark shiny reflections and behind it we can see another door and a thick velour hanging on a brass rail behind it. We sit with our parents on a huge dusty chaise longue and at last Miss Maude enters the room.

"Good evening, Edith. And Arthur. I don't think we've met before, have we?" My father smiles and looks sheepish. They make small talk, and Miss Maude enquires about my mother's aunt, who is very unwell.

Footsteps come down the corridor and one of the younger Miss Potts, Miss Lucy, comes in to join her sister. We are introduced to the sisters. Miss Maude looks me up and down before turning to my mother,

"I say Edith, isn't Caroline like you?"

"I hope not," replies my mother tartly. "She can be a handful at times."

"Oh, she can," echoes my father, for want of anything better to say. My sister annoyingly smirks and looks at them all with her big, shining, brown eyes and never says a word.

"And this is Janet? Where does she get her lovely red hair from?"

I want to kick her but dare not. I am conscious of the cast in my right eye, there since I had measles at three and a half, and had to wear a patch over the good eye to 'encourage the lazy eye to do some work'. I am aware of being quite small for my age, and of my hair being an unattractive shade of mouse.

My mother sits awkwardly. Pregnancy does not suit her and she feels unwell most of the time. She clasps her arms over the bulge in her black serge maternity dress.

My father is quite protective of her at present.

We are not shown over the rest of the school. I think it must be the school holidays, because are no signs of any other children. It is a brief and formal meeting. My mother says that in her opinion I am quite clever, but it is said as if this is something to be on one's guard against and not something to be fostered in any way.

"Is she?" asks Miss Maude, with undue emphasis.

"Well, she's always asking questions and poking her nose in," says my mother, by way of an explanation. My father comes to my rescue.

"She's always been a live wire," he says. "Don't know where she gets it from."

"And Janet's the quiet one I see," observes Miss Maude, sharply.

"She doesn't say much," offers my father, "but she's all there."

Miss Maude speaks briefly to Miss Lucy, who has been watching from the doorway. Miss Lucy has a plain, long, good-tempered face, and a smile that is a credit to whoever made her dentures. An arrangement is made that we should begin school as daygirls after the Christmas holiday, in January. No one thinks to show us round.

We are ushered out and make the journey back to the village, to our cold cottage with the slimy flagstones and the outside toilet up the garden, which we share with Mrs. Wells next door and a million hairy insects. Our father is 'doing it up' and the place is hardly habitable, but my sister and I love it.

On our first morning at Wendlesham Hall, our mother walks us to the bus stop by the pub. The nails in our shoes strike sparks from the cobbles, as we smash the ice filigrees on the puddles in the inn yard.

The cobbler who is opening his kiosk opposite the pub glares at us with disapproval. Some other children join us and we eye one another suspiciously, like stray dogs, until the bus comes. Bus rides are exciting and we treasure our tickets, small rectangular greyish cards, which the big girls put into the hatbands of the little girls in front. We get off the bus at the other end to face a long walk down the back drive to the school. This is the same lane we had driven along on our first visit. It looks different in the daylight, and the rows of cabbages, frostbitten and ragged, stand like upended dirty mops on their brittle stalks in a sea of frozen mud. These cabbages are to be our main vegetable while we are at the school. There are a lot of other children on the bus, and they mill around us asking our names and enquiring if we have any sweets. Suspicious of the approaches of other children by now, we back away and walk up the drive together.

The driveway slopes up gradually through rough pasture land, and at the top on the right is a copse which contains a deep pit in the centre, partly filled in with debris from the farm. There is something unattractive about it that does not invite a closer look, probably the carcasses of dead sheep. The lane then circles around to the right and the white gates of the school grounds appear. We follow the other children to the yard where a teacher leads us into a cloakroom to hang up our coats. Our mother, under instruction from the school, has sewn up for each of us a blue plimsoll bag with a drawstring opening, and we have new black plimsolls to put in them, marked in indelible ink with our names. After the first few days, the ink becomes smudgy and we have to guess who owns them. We have to memorise which peg we have left our coats on.

All around us, bigger children are running, laughing, shouting, banging each other with satchels and it is exhausting trying to stay out of the way of so many flying arms and legs. We do not have the regulation black velour hat of the other children; our mother had been unable to get into the town to buy them. Instead, we wear knitted woollen pixie hoods, and have to endure the taunts of the other girls until our uniform hats arrive.

Janet needs the toilet by this time, and we find them close by, behind the coat racks, reeking of Jeyes fluid. The doors do not come down to the floor, and it is possible for people to look over the tops as well. They are held shut by flimsy little bolts and I live in a constant state of panic when I have to use them because people burst in, or school hats and bags come flying over the top, or someone bangs on the door. There is something exposing and frightening about such a place, and I have dreams afterwards where I am in a toilet with no doors, trying to protect my privacy but failing, and the feeling of nakedness and vulnerability still haunts my dreams.

I stand guard for my sister on this occasion, wishing there was someone to stand guard for me.

The smell of school cloakrooms hasn't changed much over the years. There are echoes of it in shoe shops, but the smell is more than that of shoes alone. Damp coats (ours are the standard dense black wool variety common in the Fifties, faded along the seams and itchy next to the skin), give off a dirty laundry steam as they dry and the slightly fishy smell of rubber from the plimsolls mingles with the scent of leather from our satchels and the smell of grubby little bodies. It's a smell that marks the beginning and end of every school day.

A whistle blows. A teacher summons us all to line up in the yard and takes my sister and I to one side. Suddenly Miss Lucy appears as if from nowhere and leads us both off into the kindergarten, a light and airy room built off the dinner hall. I sit at a low table and thread big glass and wooden beads on to long, green shoelaces. The glass beads, which I prefer, are mostly green and brown with tiny bubbles in the glass, and there are a few in other colours, orange and blue, thrown in for good measure, and we are encouraged to thread them in colour sequences. The weight of the glass makes the beads swing satisfactorily when the lace is held up. Later, we learn a poem by Harold Munro:

'Nymph, Nymph, what are your beads?'
'Green glass, goblin. Why do you stare at them?'

In my grown-up world, whenever I see green glass beads, I have two memories; one of threading green glass beads on long laces in the kindergarten room, and one of standing up reciting the poem, aged seven, lisping because of my lost teeth, to an audience of indifferent adults.

Mostly us small children are encouraged to develop our coordination and physical skills and I spend agonised hours of concentration weaving on a serrated cardboard square, or making pom-poms, by a mysterious process, which involves two cardboard circles with holes in the centre, a lot of wool and a thick blunt needle with which we thread the wool round and round the circle. Then the magic moment comes when Miss Lucy allows you to finish the pom-pom, when the hole is almost closed up by wool and the circle is thick and fluffy. I cannot understand how this can become a pom-pom — I don't even knew for sure what a pom-pom is — but Miss Lucy's sharp scissors cut through the strands of wool, separating the two circles so that the two whiskery rings of wool come apart and then she carefully and deftly ties a strong piece of string around the centre and voila! A pom-pom is there before my eyes.

"There you are. A lovely pom-pom."

"What do you do with it?"

"You can make a yellow one for Easter and fix a little beak on it to look like an Easter chick, or you can put it on a baby's pram. Would you like to take it home?"

What would happen if I took it home? I'm not sure it will be universally admired, and I have nowhere to keep it.

"You can have it," I say, trying to sound generous.

"That's very kind of you," replies Miss Lucy. "But wouldn't your mother like to have it?" I sigh and put it in my pocket.

We make raffia tablemats; sew our names on pieces of well-fingered binca, thread laces through holes in card, and drink our milk from half-pint bottles with the familiar, waxy, collapsible straw pushed through the centre. The big girls who are milk monitors bring the crates round and Miss Lucy hands the bottles out only when we are all seated on the floor, cross-legged and paying attention. The bottles are cold and slippery; we take care not to drop them. The asthma, which had made my first schooldays such a misery, improves greatly and I begin to quite enjoy school. Miss Lucy teaches us basic phonics and suddenly reading begins to make sense. At eight, I am reading *King of the Golden River*, *Aesop's Fables*, and a terrifying Victorian picture book about ogres that ate little children; at nine and ten I am reading abridged editions of Dickens, Swift, Bunyon and classics such as *Treasure Island* and *Black Beauty*. I am well on my way.

FOUR

The biggest problem we face during that first term at Wendlesham Hall is the school dinners. It's not that long after the War, and potatoes and eggs still came powdered, and carrots, processed peas dyed a violent bile green, Irish stew and mince in gravy, came in catering sized tins. Staring down in dismay at a typical school dinner, I see a portion of tinned Irish stew containing white flabby pieces of pipes from some internal structure best forgotten, a small mound of instant powdered potato and a spoonful of the dyed green processed peas, lying like poisoned bullets in their pool of lurid liquid.

I can cope with this, just about. Food is not plentiful and being fussy about what you eat means you go hungry. The real horror is the house cabbage. This is grown on the premises, poorly washed, and boiled a long time to extract the flavour. Never in my life have I eaten anything that smells so disgusting. It makes me heave, and I know I'll have to find a way of getting rid of it.

I tell our mother about the problem, but she's not sympathetic.

"We're paying good money to send you to that school; your dinners are paid for and you just have to eat them. Ask for a smaller helping," she adds, more helpfully. I'm only six years old but rebellion burns in me like a flame. I will not, cannot, eat anything so disgusting, and it's unreasonable of adults to expect me to. It smells like the pig bins in Peterborough, putrid and nausea inducing. Janet agrees with me. Her ploy in the weeks that follow is to vomit whenever she is forced to eat something she dislikes. I can't emulate this, try as I will, and have to endure pressure, coaxing and threats.

Later, when polythene bags become more widespread, I take them to school and empty spoonfuls of the grey, stinking, revolting cabbage into my lap, hoping to land it in the bag. Then I discover an even better way of disposing of it. The dining hall is panelled, and in some places there are square holes cut into the panelling where heating pipes have been removed. I arrange to sit next to a hole like this, by threatening the occupant of the seat if she does not move over, and I keep that seat for about two years. In the course of that time, I post helping after helping of the revolting vegetable into the hole, where it falls in a sodden heap on the cavity floor. After a time, the wall begins to stink so badly that I am forced to move to another table and begin again.

My sister's bete noir is the fish, which, for a short spell, we have every Friday, as a concession to the Catholics in the school. The fish is cooked by an ex-army chef; who stays for three months and then leaves rather suddenly. Any red-blooded male surrounded by young women is going to be a risk and the Misses Potts are not married and males are seen as an alien and suspect breed of beings, who nevertheless send them all of a do-dah. The cook has developed his own style of batter, which is crisp on the outside but white and runny in the centre, with the fish slimy and half-cooked. My sister cannot cope with this at all and regularly throws up when presented with it.

As an innovation, he applies the fritter batter to spam, which works quite well and gives an edge to the cat meat texture of the Spam. After the cook leaves, the kitchen reverts to the domination of Bronwen, a grubby woman from the Welsh Valleys who does her best, but has no training as a cook. Slabs of jam tart, rock hard and doughy, begin to make a regular appearance, and semolina, in huge pink slabs is scooped out of large aluminium canteens, each scoopful looking like lurid offal. I don't know how they make the semolina, or how long it is left lying around, but on several occasions I find a large maggot, complete with tunnel, in my helping. We are told that it is unladylike to make a fuss about such things. At least we have a breakfast of bread and milk or a duck egg, or porridge before we come to school, and our mother cooks the family a meal each evening. Although she is so sick herself, it must be torture for her. Mostly, we have simple dishes for supper, like shepherd's pie or macaroni cheese or a steamed pudding. It fills our little bellies, and we are both skinny girls. Later we get really hungry. Our father always made annoying jokes about the steamed puddings, calling the jam roly-poly 'boiled baby' and the suet pudding with currents in it, wrapped in a cloth and boiled over the Aga for hours, 'bugs in a bolster'. We thought it was funny until we saw how much his comments hurt our mother, and it wasn't as if he only did it once; he commented every time until our mother gave up making these dishes, being irritated beyond endurance.

Our mother's pregnancy progresses, but she has five months still to go and she is sick all the time. Finally, the doctor puts his foot down and tells her she will lose the baby unless she goes to bed and rests completely. A neighbour agrees to take her in, and my sister and I become boarders at Wendlesham Hall. We have been there as daygirls for about five weeks.

I don't remember the goodbyes. I imagine they were difficult for my mother, though I'm sure my father saw it as a chance at last to get things done on the cottage.

He tells me later that he had no say in our care, that it was decided by our mother and her aunt, but depressed and preoccupied himself at leaving Peterborough, it's likely he hadn't the energy to object.

We were taken by our father to the school on a Friday night with our small rexine suitcases and left without much ceremony with Miss Lucy, who took us through into the dining hall, where the boarders were playing games and running about. I clutched my doll by one hand. Suddenly, before I could stop her, a fierce looking girl about my own age snatched the doll away and ran off with her. I was outraged, but no one came to my rescue and eventually the girl brought her back. The safety my doll had provided was gone; now I would only have myself to hold on to.

My sister tagged along after me forlornly. We were summoned into the kitchen, which was down a long, flagged corridor, to have a cup of watery cocoa and a slice of stale bread with peanut butter as our supper. The large ranges in the kitchen reminded me of home. There were cats in the kitchen, to keep down the mice, and we once found a cat's footprint on the jam tart. We were shown to the dormitory, by the back stairs. We were not allowed to use the elegant mahogany stairs that came down near the grand rooms we had seen on our first visit.

I remember the size of that dormitory now; it was long and had probably seven or eight beds in it. Janet's was at one end, mine in the middle. Dark enamelled steel frames, hard mattresses, white cold sheets and inadequate blankets—there was no comfort here. I was freezing. We had no hot water bottles like the other girls and this was February. There was no heating upstairs at all. I unpacked my winceyette pyjamas and took the lid off the round tin of Gibbs Toothpowder, in a solid pink block. Over the weeks that followed, I watched the dent in the centre of the toothpaste get deeper and deeper. It filled me with despair, as a daily reminder of our imprisonment.

The younger children were looked after by a matron, a kindly but strict woman whose starched white apron prevented any girl losing her inhibitions enough to imagine a cuddle, which was what we all needed, of course. Matron made us make our beds every morning by stretching the sheets over the mattress with the mattress edges curled up so that when flattened the sheet had the taut, drum-skin appearance prized by the other girls in the dormitory. Over this would go the top sheet and the thin blankets, smoothed and tucked in tight. There was an inspection every morning.

Matron had one saving grace; she liked to read aloud to the younger children before they went to sleep. The current book was a Dr. Dolittle adventure and we begged and pleaded for more every night.

"Just one more page, Matron"

"Go on, *please*." There would be a chorus of these little voices as small girls without their mothers solemnly sucked their thumbs and hugged their hot water bottles, trying to find some comfort for the long hours before morning.

Although we were so young, I can't remember any member of staff acting in a motherly way towards us, except one, an Irish teacher called Miss Prenderghast, who took my sister and I aside and sat us on her knee and brushed our hair, in a warm and motherly fashion that wasn't in the Misses Potts. Miss Prenderghast told my sister what lovely hair she had and twisted it into corkscrew curls, which sat like sausages on the top of her head. I glowered at them, wanting to smack them both with my small hands.

Although our first night at Wendlesham Hall is so cold that I get out of bed after lights out and put my dressing gown on for extra warmth, and we have trouble going to sleep in a roomful of other children, somehow the novelty carries us through that first night. While the other girls wash in tepid water from their water bottles, Janet and I try to wash in the hand basins, but the pipes have frozen and no water comes out. It's a while before anyone comes up with water from the kitchen, and we have to hurry to get down to breakfast in time for the breakfast bell.

The porridge we have for breakfast has a strange, nutty taste. It is burnt.

We make ourselves eat it. Following that, there is a small helping of scrambled egg, made with egg powder, and a plate of bread and margarine to fill us up. In the centre of the table are some large jars, which various girls own. They contain cod-liver oil and malt—*Virol* is a favourite brand—and the sweet-bitter smell of the malt is tantalising. Later, we get our own jars of this mixture. We savour the spoonful a day we are allowed with a very special pleasure and our eyes shut.

After breakfast we're supposed to go outside and walk round the grounds until the mid-morning bell rings. By this time we have found several escorts, a girl called Daphne who is a little older than us and who misses her twin brother badly. Small and vivacious, she skips around us and shows us the interesting parts of the grounds.

Where are the comforting, protective grownups we have been used to having around us? I feel very abandoned.

On Sunday nights, after tea, all the girls go into the dinner hall and sit down to write letters home. These are all read by staff before they are sent, and censored quite openly. Janet is considered too little to write a letter, but I am given a piece of notepaper and a pencil. I sit for a long time, not knowing what to write. The more I sit and think, the more homesick I become. Tears smudge the paper, and the teacher becomes impatient. I try to hold back the tears, but I feel a lead weight in my stomach that will not go away. We have been here a week.

I do not remember our parents writing to us—maybe they did, but I can't recall it in those first few weeks.

The homesickness turns to desperation. Janet begins to wet her bed. I know we have to get out of there. Three weeks after we arrive, having had no visits from our father, or news of our mother's illness, we run away. I plan it all quite carefully. I take the rexine cases from the cupboard, then put one back. It will do for my doll, Janet's teddy, and some clothes. After school is over, but before tea, we sneak off down the back drive, determined to get home to our cottage before we're caught. Of course we're found; a farmer spots us and we are brought back to the school defiant and tearful. I think Miss Maude must have told my father we are homesick, because letters begin to arrive for us from my mother.

Round about this time, we get scarlet fever. Neither of us is really ill, but we are moved to a sanatorium in the grounds, a small, prefabricated hut with a room at the side where Maisie lives. At first we're afraid of her, but she pays us no attention and we begin to take her presence for granted. But it is different when Sandra, the girl who stole my doll, goes down with scarlet fever and comes to share our hut.

Janet and I are almost asleep.

Creak.

The door opens a crack. Suddenly we are wide-awake. Two red, glowing eyes appear in the door. They begin to come closer. Someone tries to growl. Someone is trying not to laugh. Terrified, intrigued and slightly reassured by the giggle, I sit bolt upright in bed. Sandra takes her torch out of her mouth, unpuffs her cheeks and comes further into the room.

"Did you think I was a ghost? I bet you were scared."

"How did you do that?" She puts her torch back in, and blows her cheeks out. Then she turns on the light by the door. She just looks slightly silly standing there with a torch in her mouth. The effect in the dark is terrific. She comes in and makes herself at home in the third bed. Then we turn out the light and talk. Then the door creaks again, opens and shuts again, the new arrival sliding the bolt behind her. Maisie shuffles to her room in the annexe, while we lie, every hair on our necks bristling with terror, until she has gone to bed.

Now I wonder at the ignorance of the needs of young children there was, young children who were sick and far from home being put to sleep alone in a cabin in the grounds with only Maisie for company. Although we soon learned that the poor soul was not a threat to us, we would not have called out to her in the night had we become really ill, nor would she have been able to help us; she was as vulnerable as we were. When we are fit again, we are taken back to the big house and allocated beds in the dorm.

During our first few weeks at Wendlesham Hall, the weather is unrelentingly cold. There is ice on the duck pond, and snow on the road verges. I am fascinated by the ice and break off a large chunk and suck it. It tastes stale and flat. Somebody sees me and Miss Lucy comes out and sends me to bed. Why am I being sent to bed? I don't understand. I'm not tired and it's only teatime. I go upstairs; then come back down again. Miss Lucy speaks to me sternly. And just to make it sink in, she gives me a large spoonful of milk of magnesia, which is so thick and white and horrible that I imagine correcting fluid tasting like that. I realise at last that I have been punished. It was something our mother rarely did and I'm not used to it. Usually I did something, was found out, was talked to about it and didn't do it again. I had done numerous bad things in my infancy, but seldom more than once. Sucking ice was minor in comparison to these past misdemeanours.

I had, at four, pushed my windmill stick through the bars of the fireguard and lit the end, almost setting the room alight. Sharing a double pram with my sister, I threw both the shopping in the well at the bottom of the pram and the ration books out into the street while my mother was in the shop, making my sister lift her bottom to remove the trapdoor. At three, I left home on my tricycle to see what lay beyond the end of our street, and I bit someone badly at three and a half, because he pulled a nasty face at me. I was active, inquisitive and restless. Our mother played with us a lot and encouraged us to make our own entertainment. She let us help her prepare food, took us for walks, sent us on treasure hunts and read stories to us. She showed us how to look at the world and really see the small things that were there around us. Janet had found an emerald eternity ring in our cottage garden, and our mother encouraged her to keep looking. We missed what she had offered us, and found nothing of value at the school to replace it.

There is a rota for bathing, in the five cubicle bathrooms, and once a week, we wait in our dressing gowns, with our sponge bags and towels, outside the bathroom doors. Again, the feeling of having no privacy and of being vulnerable to the jeers and attacks of others is very strong. I feel very anxious that what has always been a relaxed and personal occasion with my mother in attendance is going to be taken over by someone else. Matron washes us young ones briskly with a rough flannel and carbolic soap, wraps us in a towel and moves on to the next cubicle. I feel indignant at such brisk, uncaring treatment, and my eyes sting from the soapy flannel. We are instructed to dry ourselves and she inspects us to make sure we have. That night I am warm for the first time as I get into bed.

FIVE

If it was hard for me to be away from home, it must have been doubly hard for my sister. She had already been sent to stay for a while with our aunt and uncle because our mother had to have an ear operation, and as a two-year-old, must have missed our mother a great deal. I don't remember who looked after me while she was away, but I did spend some time in my Great-Aunt Ethel's house, the house where my mother had grown up. It was peopled with elderly women: a housekeeper called Mrs. Sapsford, Miss Moore, the cook, and Mrs. Humphreys, a washerwoman from the village. Besides them, there was a gardener called Mr. Mills and Sam, who ran some pigs on my great-aunt's field. There was my mother's dog, Tuffy, and a cat that terrorised the dog, and a decrepit, old green parrot that ate hard-boiled egg and pancakes and showered parrot seed over the dining room when it was annoyed. It was a benign and exciting environment where I got lots of attention, very different from the small Peterborough prewar semidetached house my parents moved to later.

After my parents' marriage, they move into a small, thatched, rented cottage in the next village. It has a pump, a well, mice in the thatch and earwigs, and they love it. They have tilley lamps to light it and outside in the field next to the cottage there are hedgehogs that squeal when they catch their toes in the many mousetraps my father places in the outhouse. My father has a cine camera. Always a one for gadgets, he experiments with this after I am born. There I am at eleven months old, in a black and white, crackly, flickering print, wearing knickers with sagging elastic and constantly tugging them up, holding the hem of my rayon summer dress as I trip around the small garden, tumbling at intervals, but clearly delighted with myself and the world. I am not wearing a nappy, though it's unlikely I was potty-trained, and I imagine that while I am outdoors, peeing on the ground is perfectly acceptable. My mother is already pregnant with my sister, but I am my parents' firstborn and have their undivided attention for eighteen months, and my father is delighted with me. I have a little girl's face, rounded and delicate, with pale, wispy curls, and recognise in my own first child the tenderness of this soft baby roundness; the way the hair fluffs at the back of the neck, the tiny hands like starfish reaching up. Here was myself, in another form. Always an attention seeker, I appear to be dancing in the cine film and see in my second child how, very mobile at ten months, he is able to charm his brother and his parents by dancing for us.

Echoes of the past repeating, repeating.

The dancing child first displays her delight in the world with a joyous capering, captivating the hearts of her parents. Later she dances to unite the parents; with luck, they will cease the aggressive sniping and focus on her in joint admiration. She becomes the symbol of what their union has achieved. They can find nothing much to admire in each other. When I am eighteen months old, my sister comes on the scene. I am no longer on my own with my parents. I don't remember the first time I saw her, or whether I resented her, but I imagine I did. Eighteen months is not long to be the baby in the family. After she's born, my parents move with us away from the idyll of the cottage and village life, to Peterborough, and a prewar semi. I remember all of us in bed; my mother, sister, father and me, in a row, not long after we arrived. We have a doll, a dark-skinned doll with earrings and a Carmen Miranda turban, who can be turned upside down and her skirts pulled down to reveal a second doll. My memory says we have just moved, and my sister is a few months old. We are all tired, I imagine, after the journey and the upheaval of moving, and finally we are united in this strange place, without Aunt Ethel to disapprove, or any other adults to help us. The doll serves as a distraction for me. This once-only occasion of unity in our house, with all of us there as a family, is the last time I remember us all together. After my brother was born, it never seemed to happen again. The dancing is in vain.

Later, my father tells me that when he went back to Peterborough, he left us with my mother at the home of her friend, Miss Hadley, while he bought a house, as Aunt Ethel's house was not suitable for a toddler and a small baby. My mother had been Miss Hadley's companion before her marriage. My father, having found another job and bought a small house, almost decided not to send for his family. He had made a mistake in his marriage and my mother's family would never make him welcome, no matter how hard he tried. How would my mother fit in with his friends and the social life he enjoyed as a single man in Peterborough? She wouldn't. He realised he would always have to support her, and us, but would he get what he needed from this arrangement? He doubted it. And he was not in love with my mother; he felt sorry for her. He was in love with the girl he had met at eighteen and whom his parents refused to allow him to marry. I think it's likely that my mother was also not in love with him. She felt sorry for him, as he did for her. But each needed their own self-esteem; he through his work and social circle, she through her house, Somersets. Neither could easily give up something for the other, and eventually my mother won, after my brother's birth and Ethel's death left her ownership of the house. She had little else, after all. My father still had two living parents, his own money and a house. He relinquished his friends, his job, his house, to come back to Hampshire because my mother was not happy in Peterborough, and then had to abandon the house he was preparing for us when she insisted on moving into Somersets after Ethel's death.

One spring morning at Somersets, in May, I wake early and go into Mrs. Sapsford's room. She sits me beside her in the bed and reads to me from Mother Goose. Who killed Cock Robin? I want to know. These mysterious images of death are powerful and I want to understand them. I have seen dead blackbirds on the lawn with their eyes pecked out, their beaks crusty with blood, and they puzzle me. I am helped to dress by Mrs. Sapsford. I want to wear the dress Great-Aunt Ethel has made for me, a pink and white frock with frills, very Victorian in concept, and made from curtain fabric. It has a few rust marks where the curtain rings have been, but I am happy to overlook this. At nearly two years old, the pink roses are what attract me, that and the knowledge that it has been made by my great-aunt just for me. My mother thinks it hideous and says so, and that I'm not to wear it, but with my mother in hospital and several indulgent adults around me, I am buttoned into it and allowed to go outside into the garden for a while, as the other adults are not up and about yet. I stand and let the bright spring morning come to me. Soft grass, dew sprinkled with diamonds, a cuckoo, blossoms on the crab-apple, a rooster crowing, hens clucking, twitterings and whistlings and callings; small birds too swift and fugitive to identify, woodpeckers, swallows; the world is magic, brand-new and wonderful. I stand and listen and watch and wait as the dawn chorus goes on and on. Whoever is with me is silent too, and nothing needs to be said. I have glimpsed heaven. My brand-new senses are filled with wonder at the power and mystery of this vital, living world.

Everything is to be seen for the first time, with the fresh wonder of my child's eyes. A snail! Oh, its eyes pop out and go back in again! And what is this? A fragment of blue sky shaped like a ragged dome, a hedge sparrow's eggshell, lobbed onto the grass at my baby feet. Spiders trembling in their webs strung between the rose bushes, dewdrops like diadems suspended from every thread, this is enchantment.

Only when my own children were born did I recognise again the wonder I had felt at these tiny things, in a dawn made fresh and new in a country garden.

Being surrounded by so many elderly, quiet, country people is a pleasant experience; they have time, which my parents don't have, and patience.

"If the wind changes, your face will stay like that!" calls Miss Moore, catching me sticking my tongue out at my sister. Of course, I test it out immediately and am disappointed when the wind changes and my face remains the same. We are told not to pick certain flowers—stitchwort and may—because they belong to the fairies.

"If you pick may and bring it into the house, the fairies will come and take you away in the night," threatens Miss Moore, and as I bend to pick a cowslip, "How would you like to be pulled up by your hair?" I put the flower down. I hadn't wanted it anyway, really. In the fields around the house the cuckoos are calling and the apple trees in the orchard are coming into blossom. Mr. Mills, clearing the cow parsley and ground elder from under the trees stops what he's doing long enough to make me a whistle from the hollow cow-parsley stem. I blow against the bitter green stem for some time but can make no sound with it.

"It could have been hemlock," says my father, dismissing my attempts to get him to play it, and throws it in the bucket where we keep the hen scraps. My great-aunt sniffs.

My great-aunt does not approve of my father and he keeps out of her way. My mother had grown up in this house and it was to be left to her in my great-aunt's will, as insurance against my father not being able to provide us with a home, or proving an unsuitable husband. It is into this Edwardian household that I am brought as a baby and where I stay intermittently until my great-aunt's death when I am almost seven. Inside, the walls are painted dirty mustard, or papered in dull beige wallpaper, shiny with small specks of mica embossing. There are thick Turkey rugs on the floor, plum plush curtains on poles, ticking clocks and ornamental knickknacks everywhere. My great-aunt reclines on a rattan folding daybed in the porch, overlooking the garden during the day, with the parrot for company, or holds court in the drawing room, her knees covered even in summer with a plaid travel rug, and within slow reach of her gnarled old fingers is a silver-coloured cigarette box on her desk, containing Fox's Glacier Mints. I am summoned to her one day, and gently pushed through the door by Mrs. Sapsford. My great-aunt inspects me silently.

"Have you been a good girl?" I nod, wondering if this is a trick question.

Also, I am mesmerised by the drop of moisture that hangs suspended from the tip of her roman nose. When would it fall? It never did. Eventually her tired, old fingers find the sweetie and hold it out to me. I take it, watching her to make sure all is well; then I run out.

The child my parents were expecting when I was six years old, should he be a boy, would inherit this house after my mother. The baby, when it came, was indeed male. Had he been another girl, I would have inherited the property. In many ways this was a poisoned chalice, as I discovered later, and I have no real regrets, though it seems unfair that the shares became so unequal, when the property was worth almost half a million and the rest, when divided between Janet and me, was worth very little eventually, in comparison

One day, in early June, when we have been boarders for about five months, a prefect is sent to find me. I am in the Dell, a depression in the large front lawn where a few bushes grow and where some children have tried to build a den. I hurriedly leave what I'm doing and wipe my dirty hands on my summer dress, which being mauve in colour, quickly looks grubby enough without my dirty fingers on it. The prefect is brief and to the point.

"Miss Maude says I'm to tell you you have a new baby brother." It doesn't sink in. She says it again. "Your mother's had a baby. You've got a brother. Oh!" (Impatiently at my puzzled expression), "You'd better go and ask Miss Maude yourself." I go with her, collecting my sister on the way.

It's clear that although our mother is quite well, she is still weak and will need time to rest. Something else has happened, our great-aunt is dead, she died just before the arrival of my brother, and so our parents would be busy for a while.

"But you can go home quite soon now," finishes Miss Maude "So it's good news, really." We are relieved and apprehensive about this information. What will it all mean? Will our mother be sad again; as she was after her own mother had died? Will the new baby take up all her time and attention? What about our father, where does he fit into this scheme of things? Finally, in July, we go home. But home is not home anymore, we have moved into my great-aunt's house. Gone are Mrs. Sapsford, Miss Moore and the washerwoman and gardener. Mrs. Sapsford and Miss Moore, scarcely younger than my great-aunt, whom they had nursed and served so faithfully, are allocated almshouses in the village and we continue to visit them. But it is not the same; nothing was or could be again.

SIX

Janet and I are being taken to visit Mrs. Sapsford and Miss Moore. Our mother will leave us while she does some shopping in the town. Mrs. Sapsford's almshouse has an open window, and as we approach a robin flies in and comes out again with something in its beak. Mrs. Sapsford has aged since my great-aunt's death and her white hair is sticking out in small white tendrils. She is pleased to see us. We comment on the robin.

"Will he come in again?" I ask. She replies that he comes in and out as the fancy takes him. She says that if we sit down quietly, he'll come and feed off her hand. He does, and it's magic.

"Can I do it?" we clamour. She cuts up a small piece of cheese into very tiny pieces and makes us hold our hands out, palm up, and puts a tiny bit of cheese into our palm. We have to stand very still and wait. The robin sits on the windowsill and turns his head this way and that, surveying us. I want to fidget but dare not. He flies towards my hand, then turns back. I don't move. He tries again, then finally he lands for an instant on my small hand, his scratchy little feet tickling my palm, plucks off the cheese and flies out again. We stay there, while he hops back and forth, finally plucking up the courage to stand still for a second as he contemplates the titbit. We think that Mrs. Sapsford is a white witch. She even has a birch broom outside her back door to sweep away the leaves that litter her garden in the autumn.

Next, we visit Miss Moore. She is small and dumpy, with white hair in a bun. She has a bag of marbles that she has kept just for us. The marbles are glass and clay, and are quite old. One large one is ruby red, and I look through it at the world, wondering at the changes it makes. We inspect all the marbles individually. When we tire of this, Miss Moore brings out her scrapbook and shows us her most treasured possession. It is a photograph of Queen Victoria, whom Miss Moore rather resembles in looks, riding past in her carriage. Miss Moore tells me what the occasion was, but I have now forgotten it. She describes how, as a child, she had watched the queen go past and that this is a memory to treasure forever. We are suitably impressed. I know a lady who has seen Queen Victoria! There she sat, regal and composed, every inch a queen.

We liked the company of old people; they had stories to tell and a history that was mysterious and interesting. Even Gee, the mannish neighbour who lived next door to Somersets, had seen Anna Pavlova dance and could tell tales about it.

In the village were some established families of gypsies, the Bucklands and the Smiths, whose older members interested me a great deal. Old Mrs. Buckland had worked on the fields as a labourer for years, and was strong looking and imposing even when an old woman. She stood very erect and had eyes of the clearest grey, like rainwater, or agate, I used to think, and she wore a black stovepipe hat and a long coat. I tried to speak to her at the bus stop a few times, but she was a woman of few words and kept herself to herself, but she occupied a place in my imagination for many years.

Then there was Mrs. Humphreys, who lived in a leaky prefab in the village and kept geese. Mrs. Humphreys, who was related by marriage to our washerwoman, had a wispy white beard and disliked children disturbing her. We were frightened of the geese, which hissed at us over the fence and tried to peck our hands. When she came out to shoo us away, we saw that she had buckets on the floor of her house to catch the rainwater that fell through her leaky roof. When she died, the prefab was pulled down and two willow posts put up to mark the opening to the footpath that ran by her house, while a new house was built on the garden and the geese were sold. The willow posts both sprouted and took root.

The path beside her house took us up over the fields to a long incline that led down to the canal. This path was ideal for go-carts and we longed for one. For once, our father offered us some help, and we used some old pram wheels and wooden boxes to make a cart, which would take us down the incline, tipping over when it hit the flat. The canal bank itself was also an exciting place to play, as we could hang ropes in the trees and swing down over the water and back again, testing our nerves and strength.

The farmer who lived next door to us had daughters of his own and was very tolerant of us. He allowed us to use a barn loft that was currently empty but used for storing grain from time to time. We entered this private kingdom by means of a ladder, and for several years it was our private hideout. Golden dust motes twisted in the air when the light from the dusty skylight lit them up, and the floor was littered with small piles of grain where mice had stored it. We staged plays here, held secret feasts and played house. We also romped in the hay bales stored under the loft, inhaling and savouring the warm dusty smell of the hay and the scratchy bales, wrapped with their orange twine.

Some of the gypsy lads worked on the farm next door, tree felling and digging out the pond, where a small spring bubbled up out of the grass and filled the pond, creating a home for wildfowl. This pond was next to our house, and it was good to see order being restored to the field it was in, as it had become completely overgrown with bramble, nettles and dock. Our friendly farmer put some unringed pigs in there who couldn't believe their luck and who bulldozed the weeds and brambles, eating everything as they went and making huge wallows by the pond. After the pigs had done their work, he put hens in to clean up the parasites left by the pigs, and then let a couple of small ponies take it over as their own. The farmer, an ex-prisoner of war of the Japanese, was never a strong man, and his health deteriorated until he and his family sold up and moved away. A gentle man, he allowed us freedom with his daughters to join in the life of the farm.

When some of the trees on the outskirts of the wood were being felled, Reuben Smith, one of the farm workers, climbed the tree, an imposing wild cherry, while his friend chopped the other side. The weight pulled the tree over quite quickly, but it was a dangerous technique. Many of the things that happened on the farm were like this.

Later we went down to the meadows by the canal to help with the hay making, climbing aboard the trailer on top of the bales as the tractor slowly trundled up the hill with all of us on board. This was challenging, dangerous and fun.

    The hill beside the footpath was a good field for barley, or corn, which were grown there year after year. What I remember are the wild flowers growing with the barley and corn, thousands of yellow harvest daisies and corncockles, restharrow and camomile, poppies and persicaria. Harvest mice made their tiny nests at the edge of these fields. We walked carefully through these fields, so as not to knock over the standing corn, and waited for harvest. The combine circled the field, growing closer and closer to the centre. As the patch in the centre grew smaller, local lads came out with sticks and guns to catch or kill the animals that were hiding in the corn. I hated this part of the process, but curiosity to see what was lurking in the corn always made me stay. Out they would come, the stoats, rabbits, hares and mice, to be slaughtered by the waiting men. The edible catches were taken home and many families had hare or rabbit on the menu at harvest time. I found this preferable to the local hunt, with their arrogant disregard for our fences, catching inedible frightened foxes and trampling over everything. I grew to recognise that there is a skill involved in killing things swiftly and painlessly and that this is often more merciful than nature would be. This is brought home to me when my mother finds a thrush that has been killed by a car, leaving a nest full of fledglings in her hedge, ready to fly. We take in the nestlings and try to feed them with chopped up worms and mincemeat, but one by one they die, and the line of baby thrushes that follows my mother down the garden path grows smaller every day. We are very distressed by our inability to save them. We also find a bird so damaged, that barely alive, it seems better to kill it. But who's going to do this? I take a deep breath and pick up a brick, and drop it. I miss, and haven't the stomach to do it again, and the bird dies shortly after, sparing me further evidence of its suffering. Belinda's father kills his own chickens, by putting their heads on a block and chopping them off. How he performs this feat is a mystery, but Belinda assures me it's true. I watch them having their necks wrung by my grandmother, who is expert, and have to admire her competence. I think about the Nazi Party and the importance of efficiency in the gas chambers. Is it the same? I don't know.

    Death is around us as much as birth and we are curious about all of it. We see calves being born, their wet, slimy sacs slipping to the ground, to be licked off by the cow. We watch birds hatching, dogs mating, hedgehogs hibernating, foxes feeding and are part of all of it. I watch my mother breastfeeding my brother and think to myself that I want to do that, it looks so cosy and intimate.

We collect everything there is to collect from outdoors—empty eggshells, flowers for pressing, mushrooms, hazel nuts, rosehips, crabapples, wild cherries, blackberries, dandelion leaves (for our friend's rabbit), white violets, four-leaved clovers, conkers, the shed skins of snakes, coloured snail shells, feathers, pebbles, fossils and anything edible. Our pockets were always stuffed with the countryside, plus numerous other items that we treasured—a penknife, string, handkerchief (sent by our grandmother and printed with Provencal patterns of roses), and quite often, a small jar with a screw top that had once held haliborange tablets and now held the top of the milk. This was how we learned about butter. Our mother had a butter churn and made butter for the family when milk was rationed. We, copying her, put the top of the milk into the glass jar and took it with us, shaking it as we went. A small round pat of butter would finally float to the top of the jar and we would be highly delighted.

What strange little creatures we must have been. Unfriendly, self-contained, wild, secretive; distrusting adults to know what to do for the best, we were not girlish girls at all. Survival was what counted. Our parents could not be totally relied on; they had let us down too often.

My sister and I were jealous of one another, as children born close together often are. At her christening, I had misbehaved badly, and at times I hated her so much that I would take her precious dolls, tie nooses around their necks and hang them from my bedroom window, while she screamed in the garden below. The murderous anger I felt, and Janet's distress, went unheard by our mother, who could have stopped us. Feeling such intense rage and being unable to control it was frightening enough for me; for Janet, who defended herself with silent but deadly resistance, life must have been hard indeed. Now we would be described as being out of control, but in fact, we longed for some proper boundaries and it was difficult for our mother to supply these. Our father's behaviour, with his need for attention but inability to give any in return, gave us no useful models of how people might manage the anger they felt. At times he could be a real bully; at other times, when his needs were met, he would be amusing, though never loving, and this was only ever on his terms. It needed a stronger woman than our mother to stand up to him and to give him the love and acknowledgement and reassurance he so desperately craved. She had her needs too, and he didn't meet them. And yet … and yet… something in me sensed his love, unexpressed, for us all, and his hurt at being constantly rejected, even when he had brought about this rejection himself.

A snapshot: I am running in the garden in the spring wind, up and down, as fast as I can. He opens the window and looks out at me.

"Did you see me run, Dad?" He nods. "Was I running like the wind?"

"Like the wind," he replies, half smiling. Satisfied I run on. These small expressions of recognition are rare, so rare I can remember them in detail, like small jewels in the mud of our daily lives. Being ignored or bullied by him is a much more commonplace experience for our mother, and when he tries to give her credit for what she's doing, she experiences it as worthless praise. Her shrug and the way her head turns away from him say it all.

Perhaps he thought, or imagined, that if he was nice to her, he might be entitled to sex. But this wasn't what she wanted, especially as he didn't manage contraception well—neither did she—and he was open about his first sexual encounters with prostitutes in a French brothel, paid for by his mother on his seventeenth birthday. Another man would have kept quiet about such encounters, but my father was oblivious to the sensitivities of other people. Sex was a deal you paid for, and he had paid for my mother by supporting her financially and providing her with children. I imagine he knew little about the sexual pleasure of women, and probably cared less.

None of the learning of men of his class and background had involved the recognition of women as equal people with feelings and emotions like his own. The War had changed the balance between the sexes, as women like my aunt and mother contributed to the war effort and were afforded more status than those who stayed at home. Then when the War ended and the men that were demobbed came back to claim their jobs again, women lost some of the money and independence they had worked to gain. When my parents married, it was expected that my mother would give up work; especially once the children came along. This would not have been especially important, if she had maintained some status and respect in her marriage, but everything conspired against this happening. She worked hard at being a good mother, and this at least was affirmed by my father, who saw in her the mother he should have had for himself. The pity was that her motherliness could not extend to him; she needed too much herself.

"She loved you children," he would say to me later, wonderingly. "It made me so happy to see her with you. At least I got something right."

The legacy she inherited from my great-aunt gave her a small income, and no matter how poor our family became she did not return to work, a luxury few women have these days. Nor did he expect her to work. Family money was both a burden and a blessing for both of them.

SEVEN

My parents' marriage certificate gives my father's profession clearly as *engineer*. It is written in a bold and confident hand, in black ink, in the legible copperplate taught at that time. He had taken an apprenticeship at Baker Perkins in Peterborough as a young man, and worked as a designer and draughtsman there until moving south when the War started to work in a reserved occupation at Pyestock in Farnborough. It was there that he noticed a quiet, dark girl who had been sent to work in the tracing office there. It was my mother. Friends teased him about his interest, but he did nothing about it until he received a Valentine's Day card, which, his colleagues told him, had come from her. Cycling out into the countryside soon after, he summoned up his courage and visited her. She was outside in the garden and she did not greet him with any pleasure. This tall, sandy-haired young man with the large nose and narrow shoulders was not what she had in mind as a suitor, and he had taken her completely by surprise.

"What card?" she demanded, on being told he had come to thank her for it.

"This one." He produced it with a flourish. He had kept it safely in his back pocket, and it was warm and slightly creased. She looked at it with horror.

"I never sent that. It's a joke someone's playing on you. You've had a wasted journey, I'm afraid." He turned to go, crestfallen, wheeling his bike around to remount.

There was a moment's silence. She relented slightly. "Well as you're here, you may as well come in and have a drink." He thanked her, humbly, but with eager eyes, and followed her into the house.

Great-Aunt Ethel, who was weeding the beds in the back garden, looked up with surprise to see a young man escorting Edith into the kitchen and out again through the porch, where they sat on the flaky. cast-iron garden seat, unsure what to say to one another. It was chilly in the garden, in every respect.

"What does the young man want, Edith?" asked Ethel, suspiciously.

"He works in my office, Aunt," replied my mother. "He's cycled all the way from Farnborough to see me." She did not tell her aunt about the misunderstanding. My father began to have more hope, though my mother gave him to understand he was wasting his time. So many young men she had known had gone off to the War and not returned. She was twenty-seven, a virgin, and wanted desperately to have a family of her own. Could my father perhaps be the one to provide it?

My father was persistent, and called again. Ethel formed an opinion of my father that was not flattering. He arrived one day late in the afternoon, hot and thirsty. He was invited into the house this time.

It was teatime, and Miss Moore had put out one of her famous cakes, a seed cake, rather stale and with the caraway seeds embedded like tiny foreign bodies within it. The white cloth with the tatting edge was spread neatly over the walnut waterloo table, the silver-edged breadboard was in place, and the bread and butter had been thinly cut. Butter was hard to obtain and a luxury, to be spread thinly and relished. A pot of mixed fruit or marrow jam was placed next to the breadboard, and beside that, a pot of honey from my aunt's bees. Aunt Ethel still kept bees, three hives of seething furry insects, despite the fact that her sister, May, had died in this very garden one hot July day as she went to collect the swarm for my great-aunt. The bees were bad-tempered in the thundery heat and did not like May disturbing them. Despite her veil, hat and gloves, they stung her so badly that she died of heart failure. Everyone who ate my aunt's honey after that remembered the high price that had been paid for the honey. Sugar being rationed increased the importance of honey as a sweetener for everyone. Each person at the table also had a small jug of milk at their side. Miss Moore went every morning to the farm next door and bought fresh milk back in a pail. This was allocated in set amounts to all those in the house. Later I had a little black jug for mine, with a gold stripe around the rim and a round net over the top hung with beads to keep the flies away.

Miss Moore came in with a plate of bitter sliced and salted cucumber from the garden, to go with the bread and butter. Her dumpy body and clucking tongue disappeared into the far reaches of the house, as she went to find Mrs. Sapsford to tell her all about this young man who had come calling again. The African grey parrot outside in the porch gave a loud screech to remind the company he was there. My father, making a connection between the parrot and the seedcake, made some ill-advised remark about the bottom of the parrot cage being emptied to make the cake. Sensitivity was never his strong point. There was a stony silence. Nervousness made him foolish. He grinned and nudged my mother in a familiar way. He would have liked to tell a very risqué joke about a parrot called Onan who spilt his seed on the floor, but one look at Ethel warned him not to even think about it. He grinned inanely. Ethel glared at him.

"My niece does not wish to be insulted by you, young man. I have been good enough to offer you hospitality; kindly do not insult *me*. And," she added, "if you have designs upon my niece, I suggest you make them known, otherwise, you will not be welcome here again, though personally I feel this would be for the best."

My father got up and left the room, went from the house and contemplated his bicycle in the driveway. What should he do? My mother had looked very unhappy when he got up to leave. Could he turn his back on her? He couldn't. As he was debating what to do, she came running out of the house, apologising for her aunt and trying to make amends.

If only he had learned from this episode! But he never did. He never did understand that to criticise the food that another has prepared for you is a mortal sin in the eyes of most women. Later it was to become a marked feature of every mealtime.

"Oy!" he would shout at our mother as her deafness progressed. "I can't eat this. Rice looks just like maggots. Give me something else."

And he would giggle at how amusing his comments had been. Icy hostility showed plainly on the faces of his fellow diners, but he never seemed to notice.

"Can't eat pasta," he would declare, ignoring the fact that he was being given something different, "reminds me of tapeworms."

"You haven't got pasta," my mother would reply, with an edge to her voice, "so don't go on about it." It was as if she'd never spoken.

"Used to give me spaghetti when I was with my mother. Hated it then. Looks like worms. Used to give us cold mutton at boarding school; can't stick that either."

Us children, slightly nervous at an adult voicing the kind of unacceptable remark a child might make, would fidget and change the subject, watching our mother becoming more upset and our father more hateful.

My mother had an early warning when they first got together, and nothing changed after that. Ethel disliked my father intensely from that time forward, my mother's eventual decision to marry him hurt her deeply, but for my mother it was an escape from the Victorian strait jacket of life with Ethel and there was no going back.

They were married in 1943, the guests bringing butter and sweet things as presents. The War was still on and material was scarce, but my parents look sweet and vulnerable in their wedding clothes in the photographs, my father in a waisted suit that did nothing for his narrow shoulders, with baggy trousers; my mother in a white dress with padded shoulders and a small hat. She hated wearing hats, claiming her head was too large ever to find a properly fitting one. Although she did once have a small pink-feathered number with a veil, which showed off her dark hair and white skin, and which she wore to school speech days and other events later in our childhoods.

My father's family was against the marriage, recognising that my father was not made welcome in the house and suspecting, rightly, that her aunt would financially protect my mother, while my father would have to struggle to support her for no reward. They are not present in the photographs, though they may have been at the wedding.

For my father, it was the second time his family had not approved his choice of bride.

EIGHT

My mother was the fourth of four children, born when her father was forty-two, her mother slightly younger. Oldest was Beatrice, a dark-haired attractive girl, then Ted, darker still, Gordon and then my mother. The three youngest had jet-black hair, unusual for families born and bred in Lowestoft and Yarmouth. My grandfather was a clever man, also an engineer, and he applied himself to the new electric lighting that was taking over everywhere from gas. He understood about circuits and the complicated wiring needed for large municipal buildings. He originally put in the circuits for the wiring in Liverpool Street Station; he electrified the trams on the Yarmouth sea front, and generally found his expertise well in demand. My mother said he was a good and kindly father who took an interest in his children.

Enjoying some status in Great Yarmouth, he was able to afford holidays with his family in a rented cottage north of Yarmouth. The children looked forward to these times with their father, who played games with them and encouraged the boys in their cricket. One warm summer morning, he set off from the holiday cottage to meet some friends, dressed in tweed breeches, jacket and cap, and with a large punt gun tucked under his arm. They picked him up from the end of the lane and drove to the Broads, hiring the punts and stowing away the lunch hampers, guns and other equipment as well as they could. The dogs stayed on land with a handler and crashed in and out of the reeds collecting the injured duck and retrieving them. I imagine they shot the duck inexpertly, the punt gun being very heavy and the punt liable to wobble about in the water. The Broads were teeming with fish and wildfowl in those days, before PCBs and nitrates poisoned the water and coypus and mink ate what was left of the fish or destroyed the reed beds. Then the mother of all thunderstorms blew up and drenching rain fell on the party, still in their boats, and who had foolishly not gone equipped with rain capes. They must have scuttled for cover, but no one moves fast in a punt, unless they want to risk falling in. Never a strong man, this wetting caused my grandfather to take a chill; by the time he was brought back to the cottage, he was shivering. By morning he was worse. Pneumonia set in and there being no antibiotics at that time, he died soon afterwards. My mother was eight, my grandfather fifty.

Left widowed with four children to support, my grandmother became ill herself with a type of rheumatic fever, and found the job of caring for them too much to handle. My grandfather had three sisters, May, Nellie and Ethel, who paid for the boys to go to boarding school. Beatrice was kept at home to look after her mother, and my mother, poor, little, eight-year-old Edith, was sent to live with Ethel in the house that she eventually came to own. Ethel at that time was in her mid-fifties and had been a widow since her husband, a mischievous Anglican clergyman, died, also of pneumonia, in 1909. The couple had no children, and following her husband's death, Ethel had to leave the vicarage and decided to move to Hampshire, where she set up house with her husband's cousin, Mad Amy. Mad Amy had periods of lucidity, offset by periods of severe mental illness, and it was during one of these spells, religious mania coming upon her, that she tried to baptise the villagers in the duck pond, shouting that she was John the Baptist and that they must all repent of their sins and be saved. Less amusing were the occasions when Mad Amy would sharpen the kitchen knives and show them to Ethel by holding them under her nose, newly-ground edge towards Ethel's throat and utter the chilling words "You know I'd never want to hurt you, Cousin Ethel."

My poor, little, eight-year-old mother came into this household, fatherless and to all intents and purposes motherless. Sent off to nearby Wendlesham Hall boarding school away from the frightening Amy, she was faced with the almost equally frightening Maisie. It was not much of a choice, harmless though Maisie was. She had been with my great-aunt exactly eighteen months, back and forth to Wendlesham Hall, when her beloved older brother Ted contracted Hodgkin's Disease. The illness progressed fast and he died quite soon afterwards. Forever after, going away from home was linked to the death of her father, her separation from the rest of her family, (which she experienced as rejection by her mother, as she told me later), and her brother's death. No wonder she found it so hard to let go of us, believing as she did that if we left home, a terrible fate would befall us. *Out there* was full of malignant forces waiting to hurt us; there was no way we could be safe out of her sight. Ironically, on the one holiday she allowed herself to undertake with my father and my family in her later years, a phone call came to say my father's mother had died and no sooner had they arrived, then they had to set off again. For my mother, it was a vindication of everything she had believed and told us about.

Notwithstanding this fractured and difficult childhood, my mother did well at school, making the most of her excellent, almost photographic, memory; memory, which thankfully I and one of my sons have inherited. She was good at sport, art and drama and had a pleasing contralto voice. When she left school eventually, she took on a number of short-term jobs, and then went to an art college to train as a textile designer. She had real artistic ability, but sadly had no time to develop it as the Second World War intervened and she was told to join the team of tracers at the RAE, where she met my father. At some point between the ages of eighteen and twenty-eight she began to lose her hearing and by the time my brother was born she was thirty-seven and severely, but not profoundly, deaf. Hearing aids helped, but she disliked the look of them, attached as they were to chunky batteries and wires, which she tried to conceal under her lapel.

Having a deaf mother creates a deaf family, as I discover. Nobody ever really listens to anyone else, partly because it is not in my father's nature to listen, only to speak, and partly because we lack a model for communication. Also, her deafness is dangerous.

The fights my sister and I have are brutal and bloody, but if they happen out of her sight, as they often do, they go on to the bitter end, because there is nobody around to stop it, and my mother is singing as she happily chops up carrots or potatoes in the kitchen, completely unaware of us trying to kill one another in the next room. She very often mishears things, or misunderstands them and yet thinks she's heard them. Misunderstanding, she blames me for something I haven't done, but doesn't listen to my explanation about what happened. Half the time she's wrong anyway; nobody is to blame, but information not gained by her own two eyes is suspect. One evening an acquaintance of my father comes to the house. He's an interesting and cultivated man, but he doesn't look it. He's quietly spoken and unassuming. He doesn't know my mother's deaf and although he looks at her and my father while he's talking, she can't really hear him and soon goes out of the room. The man thinks my mother is finding his visit unpleasant and soon leaves; he's come at a difficult time clearly. My father, engrossed with the tale he's telling this man, does not explain about my mother. My mother has dismissed the man, dressed in casual clothes, as soon as he arrives, and has consigned him to the large human scrap heap in her mind, in which most people associated with my father are to be found. Had he impressed her with a smart suit, and being aware of her deafness, directed his attentions to her first, he would have been treated with suspicion as too charming, but she would have gradually warmed to him. To counteract her deafness, we all either speak loudly, forcefully and with a kind of shorthand, so that the basic information is received but the nuances are missing, or we speak in another language, the aside uttered in low tones, which infuriates my mother, whose sharp eyes pick up on what her ears cannot. The *sotto voce* comments are not usually subversive, but asides that it isn't appropriate to shout aloud. In the cinema, we have to risk the anger of other audience members by speaking too loudly in response to a question about the plot.

She hisses at me.

"I say, Caroline, wasn't he the actor in *The Maltese Falcon*? He's a bit of a dish, isn't he?" This is hissed in a loud and penetrating whisper and, conscious of all eyes upon me, I have to reply in a similar tone. We don't adjust well to her deafness; neither does she. Had we learned sign language, life would have been much easier; had my father been more considerate and used her ability to lip-read when speaking to her, things might have been different. But he persisted in shouting 'Oy!' at her when he wanted something, a habit my brother copied as soon as he could talk, or he shouted orders at her from wherever he happened to be. As he generally wasn't looking at her face when he did this, and she certainly wasn't looking at his, he generally wasn't heard. This is a mistake we don't make.

She's in the bedroom, with the curling tongs, trying to tame her wiry black hair, and there's a strong smell of burning. She twists a curl between the hot tongs and something hisses. She untwists it, and the curl, which now has a burnished reddish tinge to it, stands out stiffly from her head.

"What are you doing?" I am curious. She turns towards me, half smiling, half embarrassed. She has seen me come in, in the mirror.

"Trying to make myself more beautiful." She has guessed my question.

"What's that?" The tongs, like instruments of torture, lie on the glass top of her dressing table.

"Tongs, for curling my hair. Like this." She demonstrates, twisting up another curl.

"Can I try?" I take the tongs and feel their heat. She bends her head down and I catch a coarse tuft of hair at the back and twist it.

"Ouch!" I let go. She shows me how to use them properly. When she has finished, she looks in the mirror and frowns at her eyebrows. She has half an eyebrow over each eye, which gives her an elfin look, as each eye is accented like the pixies in my Mabel Lucy Atwell book. She sighs. My sister comes up the stairs and joins us. Where is my mother going? She doesn't usually dress up for things. She takes us into the large bedroom, where she keeps some of her clothes. In the drawer under the wardrobe is her collection of precious things.

"Can we look?" We skip over to the drawer. She opens it. It smells of mothballs. She sits on the floor beside us and takes the things out, one at a time.

There are some pairs of tiny calfskin and kid gloves, buttoned up the wrist, which belonged to my great-grandmother, whom I just remember. She was a tiny Welsh woman, with a miniscule waist and tiny hands and feet. We try the gloves on carefully. They only just fit us. She pulls out two beautiful old ivory fans. My sister is to have one, and I the other. There are two shawls in here too, both silk, and one is salmon pink while the other is blue. These are going to be ours too, when we are big girls. I love these treasures and feel sad later when the fan that was mine disappears and I know it is useless asking for it back. The shawl I will keep for a daughter-in-law or a granddaughter to enjoy one day.

Mostly my mother doesn't go out, except at Christmas, when the couple down the road invite us round for port and mince pies and sometimes have a New Year party for their neighbours. Sometimes her friend from the Women's Institute invites her to something and she makes an effort to look nice then. She and my father never go out together on their own in the evenings. She tries to make the best of herself, and she has thick wavy black hair, a rosy skin and neat features, and she is, in her forties, still quite slim. I think she's beautiful. She and my father are totally mismatched. Maybe she has other admirers?

She stands at the sink scrubbing potatoes. My father goes past on his way to the garage, walking behind her. She turns her head a little. He raises his voice.

"Oy! I'm going round to Monty's." She looks round, vacantly.

"Oh." Her voice is expressionless.

"I said I'm going round to Monty's."

"Yes, I heard you." He is out by the garage by now. He shouts back "Do you want anything from the shop?" She turns and looks at us.

"What's he saying?" He reappears, puts his head round the door and bellows.

"I SAID DO YOU WANT ANYTHING FROM THE SHOP?" She looks perplexed.

"No thank you. No, I don't think so." And he leaves again, banging the door behind him, and muttering. This interaction is common.

"Dad," I approach him, several years before my mother's death, "when you want to say something to her, you need to get close to her so she can see your face, then she can lipread. That's why I sit here." I sit in front of her, four feet away. My mother nods at me sweetly.

"Does she lipread?" he asks, astonished. We have had this conversation many times before, but he wilfully refuses to acknowledge what he knows to be true; that unless she can see his face, she cannot hear anything he has to say, except as a noise. Looking directly at her is to acknowledge her as a person, and this he is increasingly unable to do. Sometimes his refusal to accept and make allowances for her condition amounts to sadism, yet strangely when they have to be together and there are no other distractions, he manages to communicate with her quite well. She then finds his endless monologues and reminiscences about his life tiresome and wishes she could turn off the hearing aid and cut him out. He is like that with everyone, however, not just her, and it is a real effort for him to express an interest in other people, or to listen to what they have to say, unless it directly concerns him.

The workman, or shopkeeper fidgets, looks at their watch, the door, anything, to indicate that they want to get away, but my father is impervious to any of that.

"Dad, I think Mr. Levinson is needing to be on his way now." He pauses momentarily and follows the unfortunate man to his car, talking at him all the while.

Starved of proper conversation with my mother, partly through his own fault, he seizes on every opportunity to talk to others. He takes pleasure in being recognised as the person who chose to look after poor, deaf, orphaned Edith, who rescued her from her ferocious aunt and gave her the children she so longed for. But who she was, and is, really, he doesn't know and doesn't care. She gives him status, and that is what he cares about. Only later does he remember with a jolt that she had once been a separate person, had a career and friendships before she met him and the war intervened, and had made a decision, because she felt sorry for him, as well as needing to escape from her aunt, to spend her life with him. The jolt comes when he finally realises after her death that for years she has hated him and wished him, if not dead, gone from her house. For him she has been there, motherly and placid, as his mother had never been, and that is enough.

The son he had always wanted, my brother, is a pale little redhead, smothered in eczema and my mother keeps him away from my father, who tries nonetheless to win his affection by means of gifts and toys. His time and attention and interest are what we all need, of course, but he doesn't consider them worth giving. I see and understand the impulse behind the gifts and know it is all he has to offer. My brother and sister respond as though they are being bribed with sweeties by an unsavoury stranger; and in some ways they are, and my mother does little to change matters. She needs them too badly to insist on them having any relationship with my father. They see my mother being bullied and cling to her skirts, while I dance between them, wanting them both to be happy. The stage is set.

She undergoes another operation on her ears and once again we are boarders at Wendlesham Hall. Now it's my brother's turn to be sent away from the family to live with my aunt and uncle in Lowestoft. He is very small to be separated from her. Later my father tells me he had no say over who looked after us; it was all decided behind his back. I wish I could believe him. He was as deaf to our needs as our mother was to words.

This time we are more used to the regime at Wendlesham Hall and there are even occasions when we enjoy being there. On Sunday afternoons we are allowed to get together in the common room, to play games, put on plays or listen to music. One of the big girls has a wind-up gramophone, which we cluster round, begging to hear her records. Leadbelly, a strange choice for young girls, sings 'Goodnight Irene' over and over again. I try to fathom out the words, until someone tells me that Irene is the girl he murdered. Is this true? I am nine, and I dwell on things like that. The girl who owns the gramophone brings out her prize treasure with a flourish, a seventy-eight of 'You Can't Get a Man With a Gun,' sung with panache by Ethel Merman. Somewhere in the lyrics the words 'bloody murder' come into it, and unfortunately it was just as these lyrics were being uttered in Ethel's raucous tones that Miss Maude came into the room.

"Who owns this gramophone?" We all shuffle about looking sheepish.

"I do, Miss Maude." Gillian Wetherall owns up.

"And does your father know you listen to—music—like this?" Gillian is mute.

"My word, you girls have no idea how to behave these days. I'll take the record, Gillian, and I'll be telling your father." Miss Maude's mouth forms a pursed and wavy line. Rosemary comes to Gillian's defence.

"It's music from a London show, Miss Maude. It wasn't swearing; she was just saying it was a bloody murder, that's all." She tails off, her hand on the offending record, still out of its sleeve. Miss Maude fixes her with a gimlet eye.

"Rosemary Jenkins!"

"Sorry, Miss Maude."

"I should think so. Give me the record." Gillian hands it over reluctantly.

Later Miss Maude also confiscated Leadbelly, saying he wasn't suitable for young girls to listen to. We were left with Bing Crosby and a crying Gillian Wetherall.

The other occupation we had in the common room was writing lines.

I must not run in the dining hall. I must not run in the dining hall. I must not run in the dining hall. I must not run in the dining hall. Two hundred lines were nothing. I taped two pencils together to speed things up and wrote page after page, handing them in to the prefect, who gave them to me, with a smirk. If you broke the rules, you got an order mark. An order mark could be given by a prefect or a teacher and was usually given for being out of bounds, pushing in a queue, damaging property or being excessively cheeky. I got hundreds of order marks, mostly for being out of bounds. I was not happy to be contained within the narrow limits of the lawn and shrubbery. I wanted to climb the massive silex tree, swing from the cedar branch in the wood, tiptoe round the kitchen gardens, and explore the secret tunnel that led under the dry well at the front of the house.

The entrance to this passageway was inside the boiler house, an outhouse with a flagged floor beside the kitchens. An iron ring, if pulled hard, would raise the flag just enough to peep below and see a flight of stone steps. These led under the lawn, through the dry well about ten feet below and on, so the story went, into the town. Except that the tunnel had caved in a while ago and no one had been down there to check if it was still possible to get through. In the days when the hall had been the residence of a bishop, the tunnel was an escape route for priests, it was said.

I spent ages looking down into the dry well, wishing I could prize off the grid and go down. It was securely fastened, however, and I never did. Daydreams had to do instead.

Order marks, lines and detention seemed to be my lot quite a portion of the time. Sometimes I would instigate trouble, then hide from the consequences. Cut out spiders and insects from the joke shop would festoon windows or dangle from beams in the classrooms. Notes in invisible ink would pass back and forth. Desks moved forward in unison every time the teacher turned to write on the board. Rulers would twang as paper pellets went flying. Anything to relieve the boredom was preferable to having to endure Miss Cathcart's monotonous voice, or Miss Beavis' lecture on National Savings.

On Friday afternoons we were allowed, unless we had been exceptionally dreadful, to go into the PE hall and watch *Look at Life* films about the Commonwealth, the conquest of Everest, plucky little Gurkhas, our African chums picking cocoa beans, our Arab friends picking dates, (until the advent of Nasser and the Suez crisis), our Eskimo neighbours killing seals, all sorts of tribes-people sporting lip plugs, nose rings and neck rings, tattoos and near naked breasts. The presenter's false bonhomie and joviality were, I recognised even then, very much at odds with the real world, as the expressions on the faces of the people showed. Life was impossibly hard, but these cheery little chappies had to keep a stiff upper lip and soldier on.

It seemed to me even then the most absurd and patronising commentary accompanied these films, but at least it showed me another place that wasn't always England.

Later our mother took us to see the popular wildlife films on the circuit—*The Vanishing Prairie* and *The Living Desert,* and I remember being annoyed by the trivialisation of the subject, as the creatures were anthropomorphised and ascribed amusing characteristics, and tricks were played with the editing to make them seem to dance, or shake hands. I wasn't a serious child, especially, but I did want to find out about things without this joking, facetious commentary.

What I learned, I learned from observing the world around me, and Somersets was a good place to start.

NINE

Great-Aunt Ethel's house, Somersets, stands on top of a hill with its back to the road. She built it that way deliberately, preferring the tradesman's entrance to be nearest the road, while the porch over the front door, with its grapevine and folding doors, sheltered the entrance of official callers. From the front porch there is an uninterrupted view of the fields that border the property, also belonging to the house, and there was a stand of magnificent elm trees forming the boundary, before Dutch elm disease changed the face of England forever. These were huge, very old trees that would throw down the occasional brittle branch in a high wind and provided shelter for the pigs Sam ran in the field. Horse mushrooms grew under them in autumn, and nettles. Beyond the elms were more fields, rolling down to a stream half a mile away at the valley bottom. This stream became our very favourite place to play.

One summer my sister and I and a friend who lives nearby slip out of our house, dressed in shorts and aertex shirts, with t-strap sandals with the rubber soles that go all sticky in the heat, and take ourselves down the hill through the fields to the stream. The clay soil is cracked in the dry weather and persicaria grows with mayweed along the path. We like the mayweed as it smells of pineapple if we tread on it, and the persicaria is pink and bobbly, and we decorate our islands in the stream with its flowers. Our mother is always insistent that we tell her where we were going, and agrees to come out and stand in the field at the top of the hill and wave a teacloth as a signal to us to come home for lunch. Several fields away, knee-deep in the stream, we see her and wave back to indicate we are coming. Quite an elaborate system of semaphore develops in this way, as she appears with the cloth at intervals to check if we are okay, or that it is time to come home.

Down in the stream the water smells cold, clean and fishy, and many water plants grow there. Water plantain, which we call monkey flowers, form a clump on one bank. Loosestrife, watercress and ladies' smocks spring up randomly, with the germander, buttercups and teasels that dot the banks. The banks of the stream are clay, and we dig this out and make bowls and pots and walls for the miniature villages we build on the pebble islands we construct in the shallows. When I smell clean fresh water today in a pond or stream, it takes me back instantly to those summer days. The warm, frothy smell of polluted water is more common today, but my nose still knows the difference.

So we make islands in the stream, with palisades made from sticks and huts made from clay with leaf roofs. We sail tiny bark boats up and down from island to island and pick out minute quartz pebbles as cargo, pretending they are diamonds.

We became familiar with all the small water creatures that live under the stones and pebbles of the stream; miller's thumbs, gudgeon, small loach with whiskery heads and shark-like eyes, caddis larvae with their intricate tunnel homes made from grains of sand and twigs, mayflies, shrimps, sticklebacks and water boatmen. These we stay clear of, believing they could bite. We know where the wasps' nest is high up the bank around the corner, where the robin nests under the willow tree root, where the deeper water runs round the slow curves of the stream. The stream follows the water meadows, through culverts, under the canal, twisting and turning, collecting water from ditches as it goes. It is ours to play with and it is where we go to first when we want to play. Orchids grow with ragged robin in the brickfield next to the stream, with red clover, bistort, century and lousewort; many flowers left in a meadow whose only occupants are a few horses. For us, it is paradise. We are wild little children, my sister and I, never indoors even in winter. Great-Aunt Ethel's garden, so carefully tended, becomes an untidy mess with no Ethel or Mr. Mills to see to it. Gradually Michaelmas daisies and golden rod take over the flowerbeds, leaving their woody stalks for us to chop down in the winter and build into dens around the garden. The orchard is untended, the old-fashioned apples—codlings, Worcesters, pearmains, topple over one dry year and do not recover well. The damsons grow suckers and sprout in all the wrong places, the Victoria plum develops mildew and the raspberries disappear into the caved in cesspit, no longer in use. What had once been a self-supporting and well-cultivated garden becomes a wilderness. The syringa housing the gold crest's nest becomes leggy and ceases to flower and my father pulls it up, the circular flower bed with the tiger lilies and the ornamental cherry grows tussocky with grass, home to a nightingale whose nest we almost step upon, but it too vanishes under hawthorn and briar. The vegetable garden, the rose arch, the hen run, the rockery, the summerhouse, all subside slowly under the weight of the briars, ivy and ground elder as the garden is taken back into its original state. My mother suffers to see it become so unkempt and overgrown. The eyes of Great-Aunt Ethel still look over her shoulder.

"Aunt Ethel would turn in her grave," she would say, looking despairingly at the molehills and tussocks on the previously pristine croquet lawn. "It really is *too* bad." Sometime she shed a tear over this vanished kingdom, with its old-fashioned roses and lost flowerbeds and borders. It was too big a job for anyone to take on, but my father was usually blamed for having allowed it to become such a mess. My brother, it seemed, was to be exempt.

As children, we didn't object too much to the anarchy in the garden. We investigated it all thoroughly. Beyond the garden, our world extended to the field surrounding the garden, where Sam kept his pigs, then beyond that to the fields and meadows that stretched as far as the eye could see down the valley. Every tree was climbed, every hole in the ground investigated, every flooded meadow turned into a new playground. The year the stream flooded over the meadows where we played something wonderful happened. Magic! There were small grassy islands, silver pools and rivulets curling over the grass. Barefoot, despite being told to wear shoes, I bounded from island to island on this inland sea, ecstatic.

The fact that Somersets, our home, was on top of the hill was a great boon to us children. We could see home from anywhere we played, and we could also see others approaching. Running fast through the fields, we would lie and roll under barbed wire fences without breaking our stride, be up and off again like small mad ponies, all in the twinkling of an eye.

We were not afraid of the large sows Sam ran in our field, or of the cows on the farmland round the stream. We kept a healthy distance between any animal larger than us and its back legs, knowing from watching the dairyman in the milking parlour, who got kicked from time to time, that a good kick from an irritated cow could break a leg. One cow, a golden brown Jersey called Bunter, everyone watched out for. Her horns were sharp and she was known to turn suddenly and lunge at you if you got too close. Out in the fields, if the mood took her, she would charge with great speed from halfway across a field, and we always kept close to the wide drainage ditches, knowing we could vault over them more easily than she could in pursuit. Watching the cowman at work was a favourite pastime when we were allowed. I have a memory of one warm summer evening, when the swallows that nested in the roof of the milking shed were darting in and out and the place smelled of warm cow, dung and milk. The cows were all tethered and fastened to the milking machines, licking their salt blocks and snorting quietly, when in flew a huge insect. It was the biggest fly I had ever seen and it zoomed around in the unafraid way creatures have when they know they have the upper hand. The cows started mooing and trying to get away from their tethers. The cowman saw it and took a swipe at it.

"Drat!"

"What is it?" I asked, anxious in case it decided to settle on me.

"'Tis a warble fly—lays her eggs on their legs. That's why they want to get away." I was silent. I'd ask questions later. He had fetched his hat and was waving it at the insect, which dived and zoomed around the frightened cows. It landed on the wall for a moment and its large bronze wings gleamed in the dim light. The cowman made a lunge for it and it neatly evaded him and flew out through the door.

"Lucky her's gone," said the cowman, "Lays her eggs on them and the maggots crawl up inside them and make a lump on their backs— look at this one—he pointed at a cow's back where a raised lump was standing proud of the hide. "I'll have to cut the maggots out of that one." I recoiled.

"Ugh! Poor cows." I was glad it hadn't landed on me. Later I saw large raised lumps on the backs of some of the cows and guessed what they were. Warble flies had found them.

The old hogs were a different matter. The parasites that crept along their backs were large lice, matching the pinky purple skin colour of their hosts, and the eggs attached themselves to the fine white hair behind the ears of the pigs. Sam doused the hogs in something to get rid of them now and again, but I had happily stroked the sows and attempted to ride them before I noticed the lice.

My favourite hiding place when the world was against me was in the pig hut, a hooped wood and metal structure, with straw inside for warmth, and the old girls would lie in the dry, dusty hollows their backs had excavated, with their massive bellies and nipples lined up like cannons and their eyes with their long, white lashes tightly shut, heaving up and down in warm slumber, grunting and snorting. They fascinated me, as they were three times my size or more. I knew they could bite or jab at you with their snouts, and the sow that was biggest had worn her ring down to a lethal scimitar that could inflict a nasty wound if she so chose. But they were very gentle animals and the only real danger I faced was in being rolled on. Their own babies died by these means despite the farrowing sows being put in pens with a roll bar for the babies to hide under. Although mostly indolent by nature, they could move with alarming speed when they chose. A vet once told me that the sow had, with a standing jump, cleared a waist-high partition between her pen and the next, where he was trying to inject the piglet with something. Had he not been even faster, she would have damaged him badly. If we appeared in their field with apples, they would sniff the air experimentally and nudge each other, then gallop towards us, hungry for apples, shoving us aside to get to them and squealing to drive the other sows off.

One other animal entered our lives, Kitty, the barge horse. Kitty lived on a swampy piece of land down near the canal. She was a swaybacked chestnut mare, not used to being ridden, but we tried, and got a good kick or two for our trouble. Kitty, like her owner, Mark, was getting on in years, and she was put on light duties. This meant that she towed a few barges from time to time along the canal when there were rushes to be cut or wood to be shifted. It was hardly exhausting work but Kitty would work for a while, then call it a day, wade into the canal and have a leisurely soak, while she munched the interesting canal-side plants.

"Come on, girl, up ye get." The lad with her would tug and pull. Kitty obstinately stayed put until she decided her tea break was over, and the lad whacked her on the flank, climbed back into the barge and set off once more. It was easier with two men, one to lead the horse, and one to steer the barge. Once, barges had gone up and down all day, loaded with china clay for the pottery at Basingstoke in one direction, goods bound for the Thames ports the other way, along with coal, timber and animal feed.

The lives of everyday creatures were inextricably mixed up with our own; we were as familiar with the pig in the field as we were with our baby brother, indeed the pigs seemed more interesting to me than my brother, who was not allowed to wander out of sight, even if we were with him. My mother's hostage, he was frequently ill and ate poorly, resulting in chronic constipation and the inevitable syrup of figs, or worse. His screams escaped from behind the closed doors of the bedroom where my mother and a nurse attended to him.

"Why is Douglas crying?" My mother looked at me with irritation. Why must I always question things?

"Because he has a tummy ache and the nurse is making it better."

"How is she?"

"Stop asking questions. Have you done your homework yet?" I turned my head away and went downstairs. I found a secret book, one that had belonged to Great-Aunt Ethel. The cover was uninteresting, black with *St John's Ambulance* written on it. Inside, men were bandaged from jaw to crown, arms were splinted, sick rooms fumigated. There were illustrations of douches, enema bags, breast pumps. This was a fantasyland, and my brother had entered it. I shuddered and put the book away.

Somewhere, somehow, my brother the hostage was trying to wrest control from my mother, refusing to eat or defecate, and in doing so, he risked losing the only security he had, a precarious security, as he had, like us, been separated from her while she had yet another operation on her ears. None of the operations worked, though one gave her back her hearing for several hours, only for it to be lost the next day. How cruel of fate to play such a trick on her! She came home, suffering from vertigo and sickness, too ill to do anything but sit or lie down. It was then that Mrs. Gadsworth came into our lives, a blessing we were badly in need of. She took over the housework, listened for my brother when he slept—there were no baby alarms then that my mother could have heard—and instilled some manners into us. She wasn't afraid to tell us straight what was what.

"Don't walk on my clean floor 'til her's dry," she insisted as we hovered outside the tiled kitchen, waiting to cross the floor. A woman of impeccable honesty who worked hard all her life supporting a delicate husband and elderly mother by scrubbing other peoples' floors and toilets, she instilled in me a deep respect for the whole army of women everywhere who do what they have to do to support themselves and their families and remain cheerful and steadfast, and who are exploited shamefully by contractors and agencies, in hospitals, schools and large corporations.

Mrs. Gadsworth had self-respect and viewed the world with a straight, direct gaze that was completely honest. She was exactly what our family needed.

TEN

Early July, and we are eight and ten years old, desperate for adventure and fun. We ride our bikes around the neighbourhood, climb the horse chestnut tree at the top of our drive, even though it doesn't belong to us, and make dens in the garden. We have few friends; our mother forbids us to mix with the village children. Amy, from the next village, goes to our school, and although our mother, who is a snob, criticises her Wirral accent, she is allowed to be our friend. Sandra, who is my sister's age, comes round from the farm next door, and Belinda, whose mother is friends with our mother, also comes round from time to time. We treat Belinda badly and take a sadistic delight in taking her to places where she will fall into mud, scratch herself on brambles or become paralysed by fear whilst climbing a tree. Not physically adventurous, Belinda to her credit attempts to keep up with us, but usually fails.

There is a culvert under the canal, carrying a stream. The stream is usually shallow, but drops into a deeper pool at one side of the culvert, in the direction of the water flow. The first time we find this culvert, we have to skirt around the side of the pool to peer along its echoing length. A small bright circle of green shows at the other end of this telescope. Liverwort and moss grow inside the entrance in overlapping layers. Do we dare to go through this tunnel to the other side of the canal? One thing prevents us: spiders.

I go first. I am just too tall to go through without crouching. I try not to touch the sides of the tunnel, which smell of wet metal and have orange streaks of rust and hard black bolt-heads at intervals, which catch on my arms. The smell is clean and powerful. There is river water, (fishy, sharp) corroded metal (clanging at the back of the nose) and a combination of other smells coming from the woods I had left and the water plants awaiting me on the far side. The smell of the woods was warm and nose tickling, while the plants carried a whiff of spearmint and watercress. One other smell came drifting through, a smell that permeated most of the places we played—mud mixed with clay. The greasy, primitive fumes of the clay filled our nostrils often. The clay formed the banks of the stream. The greasy smell was due to the heavy vegetable oil deposits in the clay, which shone in small rainbows on the top of swampy stagnant pools. The woods alongside the canal were thick and boggy; dangerous to enter, the willows growing at crazy angles as they aged and toppled over. The soft sucking mud in the sump expelled bubbles from time to time.

We didn't like these woods; there was something sinister about them. Even the ducks didn't nest there. Dogs knew better than to venture in. We knew our way through these woods, along an old cart track, built like a causeway to carry clay and bricks between a kiln in the field and the village. We also knew from experience that in a wet field, the side of the stream is drier than the surrounding land, and there is usually a path along it. Animals made these paths sometimes, and these trails would veer off to one side when a ditch joined the stream, until a crossing place was found, or there would be tufts of hair or fur on the barbed wire where the animal had ducked underneath. We followed these trails with interest and became good at tracking and reading the signs of the countryside.

The culvert opens out into a field on the other side, and I reach it with relief and a cricked neck with my boots full of water and light dazzling my eyes.

Janet and Belinda follow me. Back at the pool on the side we have left, some boys have arrived and call to us through the culvert. This is good fun and the yodelling and calling goes on for some time. Belinda, who is overcome with her own daring, does not want to go back through the culvert, but some adults are spotted coming along the lane ahead of us. Belinda knows one of them and is afraid they'll report her activities to her parents. We scuttle inside the culvert again and shuffle back along its length against the flow of water, wetting the insides of our boots again.

The boys are catching minnows in the pool, using bread and spitballs and tiny hooks. They want to use the minnows for bait to fish with in the canal above, where the big bronze rudd and steely pike lurk in the shade of the hazel and ash trees that overhang the canal. The boys are intrigued by our antics and indulgently show us how to catch minnows. The biggest boy puts his hand in his pocket.

"Show you something?"

"What is it?" I go nearer. Janet stays out of range. Belinda is drying her feet.

"This. Not scared, are you?" He has in his hands a small grass snake, about six inches long, twisting its neck around. The yellow patch on its head and olive skin are beautiful. I know at once what it is, I had seen one very close to in our garden, as I sat on top of an empty beehive watching a small mouse. The grass snake unravelled itself below me on the warm shelf where the bees came and went. The shelf was littered with the dry furry bodies of dead bees. The snake was shedding its skin and didn't want to be disturbed. I crept away silently.

Our mother had told us the difference between grass snakes, slowworms and adders when we were tiny, by showing us pictures and taking us for walks where we could see the real thing. I can still walk along a riverbank and find you a snake or a lizard, while others would pass by and see nothing. She taught me to look, see and distinguish from its surroundings everything that lived and moved around us.

The boy holds the snake out to me, watching me for signs of fear. I reach out to touch it but the snake messes in his hand and he drops it with a curse.

"Soon get another," he says carelessly, as the snake vanishes into the grass.

"Where did you find it?"

"Got 'im yesterday when my dad moved the grass cuttings. There are loads in our garden," he adds boastfully, wiping his hand on his shorts. The boys move off with their minnows and settle themselves at the side of the canal to fish in earnest. We sigh and head for home.

Adders are common along the less used banks of the canal and on the heath land where the clay ends and the sandy soil takes over, on the other side of our village. Adder Common is a popular footpath for villagers, and adders have bitten several dogs. We have learned to be careful.

There is another pool in the stream, on the other side of the small bridge that carries the cart track over the field. This pool is deep enough to swim in. We can just swim, but know we'll get into trouble if we do. Belinda, who thinks of herself as a water nymph trapped in a human body, is eager to go in. She puts one white leg into the shallow end.

"Ugh!" Small shrimp like creatures scurry over her feet, a whiskered loach fish is startled into leaving its sanctuary under the bank and darts into the deeper water. Belinda gets out, afraid of what might be in there. But the idea is lovely. Regretfully, we leave it behind.

ELEVEN

My father has lost his job. He fell out with the foreman, not liking being told what to do. This is my mother's opinion and she goes around the house with her mouth pursed up, wondering how we'll manage now there isn't a regular wage coming in. Father is determinedly cheerful. He leaves the house early one morning and comes back, announcing that he is going to be a Betterware salesman. My mother is appalled. It's a lower class occupation at best. How can he think of such a thing? He is full of it: all the gadgets and contraptions for getting dirt out of hiding places. He brings home samples of brushes, polishes and cloths until my mother wants to scream, but we all know he's whistling in the wind. At first, he sells a bit to people he knows who take pity on him. There's a depression on and people try to help one another out. But the goodwill runs out eventually and he goes farther and farther afield, selling housewares to bored women. My mother takes her gold locket and tries to pawn it to pay the milkman. My father finally gives up and sits at home, moping and depressed. Eventually he decides to be a secondhand car salesman and borrows money from his family fund to buy a small garage in the village. He will sell petrol, repair cars and sell them on. His large, unbiddable fingers are no good at working with intricate car parts in greasy surroundings, so he'll hire Ken, who becomes a partner in the firm. It's just as well Ken knows what he's doing, because my father doesn't. Ken is always covered in oil and grease, but he's a nice man and a good mechanic. My father sits listening to opera in the office and lets Ken do the work.

All this time, we have very little money. My sister and I have to wear secondhand clothes, and our school uniforms are tatty and old. We get teased at school. Bundles of secondhand clothes arrive from our aunt, who has a friend whose daughter is our age. We leap on them and pull the contents out before our mother has had a chance to look at them. Pink nylon with ruffles! Blue and white stripes! We can't wear half the clothes because they're not suitable for the rough and tumble lives we lead. Perhaps once a year at a birthday party we get to wear something pretty, but at home, it's either school uniform or shorts and aertex shirts.

To avoid the tensions of the house, we go out whenever we can, and our favourite activity is to go on the canal in a canoe or a rowing boat. As a group of little girls, dressed in shorts and aertex shirts, at home on the water, we are an attraction for the prowling men who pop out of the bushes along the canal while we are quietly rowing along, minding our own business. The dog that comes with us is perhaps a minor discouragement to them, and we, being safe on the water, don't bother about these sad old misfits who loiter about the canal bank. When I was thirteen, this changed, but this time I was on my own and on the canal bank. Luckily, having a keen sense of self-preservation and not being afraid to defend myself, I escaped from what could have been very serious harm by kicking him and running for my life. My parents, for once united by this event and the interest the police took in it, behaved with remarkable commonsense and bought me a dog. But they did not dwell on the incident and understood my fears. Another younger girl in the next village was not so fortunate and was subjected to a serious assault before escaping. The young man, a gardener, was placed in Broadmoor, where he subsequently hanged himself. This fact upset me greatly, although I did not feel personally responsible for his suicide. I had played a role in his life, and the fact that he was now dead was shocking, because it was also a relief. And by the time of the suicide, I was not far off the age he was when the incident occurred. How young he had been, and what a senseless tragedy his life turned out to be. I learned that pity and compassion are healing, whatever the circumstances. Later I work with several sex offenders, though not by choice, and rediscover the pity for the man, though condemning the deed.

The dog we take in the boat belongs to the girl on the farm next door, Mandy, and is a fat Black Labrador called Sheba. She is a liability in the boat, for she gets excited and runs down the boat, trying to reach the object she is interested in—usually another dog. By transferring her considerable weight, she destabilises the rowing boat so that it rocks about dangerously. Sheba thinks nothing of throwing herself off the boat if the other dog is particularly handsome, and swimming to the bank. This is inconvenient, but we trust her not to wander too far away, and she never does. Our mother feels safer when we go out with Sheba and Mandy, and Janet is upset when the farm is sold and Mandy and Sheba move away. Mandy had been her special friend. Friends are in short supply in our village.

Back at home, things are not going well in the garage business.

One day Ken comes into our kitchen. Our father is in London fetching some motor parts. He'll be back later, all excited about what he's seen and the exotic street life of Balham. Ken doesn't get to see any exotic street life. As usual he's covered in oil and grease and he apologises before he sits down, taking care to put something on the chair first so as not to dirty it. A tall, thin man, Ken has lovely eyes that are pale moons in his grease-streaked face. Our mother looks at him with compassion. She likes Ken. He lives in an extended prefab in the village with his five children and his wife, whom he adores.

"Edith," says Ken, "it's a bit awkward what I've come to see you about." He shuffles uneasily in his seat. My mother looks anxious and turns up her hearing aid. She's ready to receive him. She looks carefully at him, watching his mouth.

" I wonder if you could have a quiet word with Arthur for me?" She nods slowly. She's heard that all right. "The thing is, we've got people owing us money. Arthur's doing the books and everything, but he's not very keen to chase up the people who owe us money. It's difficult ..." He tails off. My mother sighs and thinks what to say.

"I'll talk to him, Ken," says my mother eventually. "Who is it that owes you money?" Ken looks relieved. He takes a deep breath, reassures her.

"Don't you worry about that, Arthur's got the details. I just thought I'd come to you because you know what Arthur's like, and frankly, I don't know how much longer I can work for him if he's not able to pay me. I've got the kids and Hettie to think about, you see. It's different for Arthur." He means by this that our father has family money to fall back on, and he doesn't. Our mother is well aware of this.

"How much does he owe you?"

"I'm owed about three weeks. Hettie and I, we can't live without a wage coming in." Again he tails off. "You'll talk to him?"

"Ken, you're not to worry, I'll see you get your money." He believes her. "I'll talk to him, Ken, but it may not do much good. You know how he is."

She looks worried, and when she's worried, her eyebrows raise a little. They're different from his eyebrows; they end in the middle like the pixie eyebrows on my kewpie doll. Her voice always comes out louder than she wants it to, but he's used to this. He gets up to leave.

"Sorry to have to come to you with this, Edith." She doesn't know what to say. In the end she nods at him.

"Bye." She sighs and gets up to put the supper on.

We try to hide when my father comes home, but are able to hear what's going on. Of the two, my mother is the better protector, but she's vulnerable herself and she doesn't know how to help our father. He shrugs it all off, but she insists Ken gets paid and my father is forced to borrow money from the family trust to pay him.

Life gets more difficult. We hide when creditors come round; pay the milkman in stamps because there is no money in the chicken-on-a-nest on the dresser, where my mother always keeps her change. She becomes distant and distracted and finally takes her most precious piece of jewellery, a gold mourning locket with seed pearls, to the pawnbroker in town again. Disgusted by the paltry amount he offers for it, she brings it home again and thinks of something else.

Eventually Father is forced to admit that the garage is not making money. He will have to sell. What next? He is forty years of age and nothing has gone as he hoped. He becomes very depressed and bad-tempered, being indoors all day and feeling trapped in this house he hadn't wanted to live in. My brother is four years old, a timid, anxious child prone to chest complaints. He is small for his age. My father pays him clumsy attention, when he remembers he exists, but he dislikes the fact that he clings to my mother. My brother hides in her skirts and becomes the buffer between the two. The tension in the house is unbearable.

Finally my father talks the family trustees into giving him some money to start up a business on the South Coast, a dog grooming parlour, and Nick the Greek comes into our lives.

Soho on a Saturday night. My father has taken us to meet Nick the Greek. My mother distrusts him instantly, but goes along to protect her family. The bright lights are seductive and the wet streets reflect the lights in wobbly doodles, right up to our feet. We go into a cafe run by one of Nick's relatives and my father orders coffee for himself and our mother. We have Kia-ora. My brother has been left with the babysitter this time. We gaze at the Espresso machine, belching steam and hissing, and the Formica tables and counter, black with a gold trim.

Nick smiles at us with his crocodile teeth and my mother glares back, unwilling to be friendly. He tries his best to charm her, but she simply won't be charmed. Father goes ahead anyway and sets up a business on the South Coast and makes contact with an old girlfriend again down there. My mother is furious. It's the last straw. With an astounding lack of tact, he invites my mother to meet her and naturally she refuses. The old girlfriend anyway refuses to part from her husband who is jealous and dependent, and my father has to cut his losses, realising that he and my mother are doomed to stay together.

My father tells me of the meeting with his girlfriend. My father and Nick the Greek are walking along the seafront, congratulating themselves on the acquisition of a shop that will be the poodle parlour. They will cater for the pampered pooches of Bournemouth, make money and have fun.

Suddenly my father stops short. A woman is approaching, a woman whose walk and outline he recognises immediately. She notices him and slows down, her face questioning him to see if he recognises her.

"Joan!"

"Arthur! What are you doing here?"

They make small talk; can't begin to say the things they want to say. Afterwards Nick says to my father:

"You and that woman, you really love one another. I can see it in your eyes. This is sad for you." My father, telling this tale, chokes a little. He is supposed to love my mother, but she doesn't want what he has to offer. He and Joan should have married, he tells me. His family objected, saying she was common. He was in love with her, at eighteen, and it had been impossible to forget her. Now it's too late.

The poodle parlour too fails when Nick vanishes with the takings and the woman who runs the parlour disappears with him.

It's different for my mother. She tells me later the marriage was a mistake. She dislikes sex, tells me my brother's conception was an accident, later had a miscarriage and hates my father for not having managed contraception more effectively. He has not managed anything well, it seems. When I am nineteen she tells me that the best contraception is the little word *No*. It's too late for me by then; I'm already exploring the possibilities of condoms, caps and pessaries, since I don't want to get pregnant, but I can't identify with her attitude. My closest friends are male; sex is exciting, no way am I going to get pregnant. I knew it all, or so I thought.

Ominous sentences starting with "Men are all ..." and "Nice girls don't," all added to the guilt. Then there were warnings about being too clever. "Men don't like women who ..." and "You want men to respect you." I wasn't sure about this. What did respect mean? I wanted equality, nothing more, nothing less. In my experience, one didn't gain respect by being passive and ladylike. I had had to fight for respect.

I realised later she had had no father around to give her any blueprint for how men and women might be together. There was little emotional intimacy, little togetherness with my father, and he lacked the sensitivity to see how he might help her to get close to him. He could give her babies, if she allowed him near her, and he knew, or thought he did, with cast-iron certainty that she wanted this more than anything else. But the babies came at a price; each of our births trapped her with him more. Later, my brother and sister became trapped as hostages in the doomed house.

Dimly my mother was aware that a separation would destroy my father; what she wasn't able to see was what it would mean for her.

Without him to be angry with, the multiple losses in her life would be dangerous destabilising elements. It was easier on the whole to carry on the battle with my father.

There were some reprieves; odd occasions when other people were present and they had a truce. The exchanges between them on these occasions seemed false, with him laughing a lot at his own jokes and her trying to excuse his behaviour. He embarrassed her a great deal, with his insensitivity to the feelings of others and constant need for attention. She squirmed when he revealed sensitive, personal information about their lives, told people about his boarding school experiences, when he droned on about car engines, Latin American music, bandonians, bottled fruit, his friends in Peterborough, or showed them his varicose veins. He was totally unable to carry on a two-way conversation with anybody; he could not allow their reality to creep into his world. He might remember their occupation, if they told him, especially if they were engineers, but he would never ask them for information about themselves, and he would never respond to or notice their mood, feelings or emotional state. To this extent, he was more handicapped than my mother, who coped with her deafness in her own way and managed adequate conversations with people much of the time. With people that my father got to know well, he was able at times to exhaust his attention-seeking tactics and become more himself. It helped not to pay any attention to behaviour that was odd or unsociable, and to pay close attention when he showed a more normal response, which he could occasionally, given encouragement. He had very little of this at home.

My father often became uncomfortably aware of his own feelings of misery in this hostile household, even though he was unaware of the feelings of others around him. Things didn't improve. My leaving home eventually gave him fewer avenues to express his misery.

Later he would phone me.

"I feel so miserable, Caroline. I feel like ending it all."

"I'm sorry to hear that, Dad. What's brought this on?"

"It's awful here; you have no idea. My grandmother warned me not to marry Edith; she said I'd regret it. She was right."

"Would it help to talk it over with someone?" Knowing he won't kill himself; won't get help. He just wants to share his misery with me.

"No, I'll be all right. It's so ruddy hard when I try and try and still get nowhere."

"Have you got any friends you can talk to?"

"No, they're all dead now. Old Raymond and Ruth, they were good friends to me, friends to Edith too. They're both dead. Pity." He goes quiet.

"I don't know how I can help you, Dad."

"Never mind. I'll manage." Telling the other family members about his distress brought nothing but a stony silence.

"He's only got himself to blame," was the response. Which could have been true if he had been able to help himself, but I had long realised that he was unable to do this unless supported. My mother felt loved by her children, though she fought with me because I wouldn't automatically side with her against my father, but my father felt loved (and was loved) by no one. The ex-girlfriend assumed huge fantasy proportions but although there was continuous correspondence, they did not meet again.

I became used to these one-way conversations. He would never ask how I was, or enquire about anything I did, or follow up any comment I made about his grandsons, our work, health, lives or happiness. It was as though no one else existed, except himself.

Reading with a shock of recognition many years later a paper on personality disorders, I realised that the characteristics listed were his, all of them, and that he was typical of narcissistic people who have been neglected and emotionally abused in early life and who are forced to employ any means to guarantee their survival. Other people only matter if they threaten this survival, which is based on not being abandoned.

Changing his mind and disregarding the plans of others, magical thinking, the notion that others are there for the sole purpose of serving his needs, basic lack of empathy, the need to prove himself right, superior and powerful in relation to others—these were all his characteristics. Yes, he could be hateful. So why didn't I hate him as my brother and sister did? Sometimes his smile told me he loved me. Sometimes, if I entered his world as closely as it was possible to do, it was clear he was grateful for the company. He had no one else. I gave up expecting that he would ever share my world; he simply wasn't interested unless something I did shed glory on him. Living with a narcissistic partner or parent, to survive, one has to insist on the reality of one's own feelings and their legitimacy, and insist that they are respected. This is hard work.

At times he can be entertaining, good-natured and willing to help, when he feels valued and attended to. But at other times, most of the time, when he is not the centre of attention, he is irritable, bullying, bombastic and cruel. Most of the time, he is just Dad, or 'your father' and many of my friends have worse parents.

TWELVE

Like most of my father's enthusiasms, keeping bees was bound to end in disaster. This is the garden in which Auntie May died of bee stings, and my father is not going to let that happen to him. The hives are neatly arranged and my father has repaired them. They are a suitable distance from the house. I like to go and sit on top of the hives when the bees are not too busy, and watch their comings and goings.

It is July, and thunderclouds pile up on the horizon. The bees are grumpy and overcrowded. My dog comes out to see what's going on and a bee zooms down low onto his muzzle. He becomes hysterical and bolts. Suddenly the garden is full of bees, flying low and filling every inch of air space. I run for shelter and try to get the dog to come inside. He, panicking, runs through every bush and shrub, trying to scrape off his tormenters. Finally, he comes inside and we hold him down while I pick off the bees and bathe his stings, which turn out to be mainly on his muzzle, as they have been unable to sting through his thick hide. He feels very sorry for himself, and there is a pool of dribble on the floor under his mouth in which several bees are drowning.

I cautiously go outside again. The air is quiet. I look round, and see a large plum pudding in the apple tree, which on closer inspection turns out to be the swarm, seething and alive. No one knows where my father is, but the swarm is valuable and must be taken. We phone the family at the other end of the village, and Dolores comes trundling up on her bike, bringing her bee skep and hat. Donning the hat, but disdaining any other protection, Dolores holds the skep under the ball of bees and then gives the branch they're on a good whack with a stick. The weight knocks them off neatly into the skep, she puts the lid on quickly and cycles home again. My father is very pleased and rehouses them at once. Later in the year, he tries to extract the honey. He puts on the full regalia and looks like a Martian as he strides out to collect the honey. Our mother watches fearfully from a window. Despite the smoke gun and the protective clothing, my father's clumsiness angers the bees and he is inside the house again, yelling to my mother to come and take the bees out of his clothes. He has a dozen bees crawling about inside his veil and down his neck. She has to remove them all. We watch, fascinated and wanting to laugh. He goes out again and this time returns with the honeycombs, each comb neatly covered and capped with wax. The smell of honeycomb is wonderful, and we watch while he slices off the caps and puts the combs into a drum, which is turned to extract the honey. The house is a mass of stick and sweetness, and we chew the wax combs to extract the honey. He sells the honey to a collective and for several years, the bees flourish. Then one winter he forgets to feed them. Deprived of their honey and with no additional food to sustain them, they die. The little bodies are piled in small furry, mouldy mounds when we open the hive. The field mouse who has over wintered in there along with a shrew do not like being disturbed. There is a nest of moss and tiny grasses, which we open, revealing minute naked pink babies. We close it up again quickly.

My father tries again with the bees. This time the swarm he puts in is already angry and sentry bees are posted to fly around the hive at a distance, which means that all visitors to the front door are swiftly chased away by angry insects. After the third visitor is stung (Sam the pig man, on the nose), my father moves the hive further away. These bees are not friendly like the first ones. I go out wearing perfume one day and they head straight for me, expecting, I suppose, nectar to go with the scent. Disappointed, they chase me inside again. Everyone gets stung. It's not funny, and my father neglects them until they die and the hives keel over and rot away. All that's left are the perforated zinc trays that the bees use as a base to build on.

The wasps in the garden are a different matter. I find the wasps' nest by accident, under the lilac tree in a hole under the ground. The wasps are sucked into this hole in large numbers at dusk, and Mr.

Mills says he'll have to kill them. But before he does, another predator gets there first. The nest is excavated and the lawn is littered with dead wasps and papery bits of nest. My mother tells me that a badger dug up the nest in the night to eat the grubs. The sharp marks of its claws are on the grass around the hole. I find this all very exciting.

The wasps, undiscouraged, set up home in the loft and make a beautiful paper lantern of a nest, quite large, which crumbles away next winter when my father goes up to look at the stuff stored up there and grumble about it. We learn to live with these creatures, seldom get stung and find they add piquancy to our lives.

Wintertime, and I am ten. We have friends who live a mile away at the other end of the village. They live in a warm cottage smelling of cats, and because there's no electricity there yet, there are tilley lamps hanging from the kitchen beams and an outside toilet that stinks of Jeyes' fluid and pee. But the kitchen is warm, with a range warming the whole house and baskets of puppies asleep in a basket in the corner, their small bodies rising and falling as they snore and slumber. Cats prowl round on the work surfaces, and our friend's mother, Josephine, magnificently large in a stained, red satin dressing gown, tends to them all. She cooks beautiful small cakes, my mother says, though if you saw the kitchen, you might not want to try them. Bella, her pug bitch, stands in the doorway, yapping and showing her ridiculous teeth, which stick up from her lower jaw like those of a deep sea fish.

We stay in this cottage, with its lumpy beds and cats everywhere, feeling a cosiness that is missing from our own home, while our mother is ill again. Josephine and her daughters are welcoming, and the mentally handicapped sister-in-law who lives with them from time to time, and is unable to speak clearly, is not frightening to us, as she sits and embroiders by the fire and smiles lopsidedly when we approach. The cottage is on the edge of the woods and surrounded by kennels housing animals that Josephine is caring for. The cottage is very old and has wattle and daub under the plaster in some rooms. There are ghosts there. Josephine cares for my mother when she is sick carrying my brother, and my mother tells us afterwards that in the small bedroom where she was being nursed, she felt an evil presence in the room with her and went cold with fear but was unable to get out of bed or shout for help. It's a house where the worst illness people suffer from is impetigo, and where the fragile, but smiling, sister-in-law is tolerated and cared for. Nobody shouts or seems to lose their temper, instead, they huddle round the Aga, waiting for food or play games on the big table by the light of the tilley lamp, shooing away the interfering cats from time to time, or tending to the puppies. I don't remember a proper bathroom there; perhaps there wasn't one. Many cottages still had a pump or a well for their water. This one had a deep well, in the centre of the lawn, and the water was pumped up by a generator, which throbbed all night and yet was strangely comforting to hear, like a deep heartbeat in the depths of the house.

The family kept bees, as my father did, and from the honey they made mead, which they kindly gave us to drink at Christmas. The house, warm, muddled bird's nest that it was, could throw up unlikely supplies of things we needed. One winter, when it was very cold and the canal froze hard and dry, we were desperate for skates.

Suddenly a wooden box full of ancient pairs of skates materialised from the outhouse; old, pointed-toed, leather lace-up boots with skates on, lethally sharp and more suited to the narrow Edwardian foot than our fatter, wider, nineteen-fifties feet. They were almost museum pieces, but we crammed our chilblained feet into them and skidded across the ice, joining the other local children and the odd adult who came to see we didn't fall through. We conned somebody's mother into giving us a brazier and we took an oil lamp to hang from the tree, so that we always had a point to go back to. The zing of steel on ice outside at night brought a tingle to the blood, and we raced along, seeing fish under the ice, darkly flickering below us. Later I read Wordsworth's poem about skating and understood exactly how he had come by this vision of exhilarating movement and sound. Several boys had joined our group of friends by this time, and there were some tender romances and delightful encounters, all very innocent and touching. We were only fourteen and fifteen and the world was a very different place. Childhood lasted for longer, but there were some of us for whom it became irksome and some who never escaped from childhood. Under the surface there was resistance and rebellion. James Dean showed the way, others followed. We were entering the age of Rock and Roll.

THE ENGINEER'S DAUGHTER

At boarding school again, when the arrangement with Josephine breaks down, we have to adapt once more to life away from home. It is Sunday, and we boarders have to put on our black velour hats and black woollen coats to walk around the freezing Hampshire countryside after church. We walk in a crocodile, in pairs, and the word amuses me. I walk with my sister; then have to swap and walk with a girl called Margaret Rose Susan Taylor. Margaret Rose is small and dark and very pretty, but has a spiteful nature. My first meeting with her had been at breakfast when she bounced over to my table, slid along the bench beside me and pinched my leg with a viciousness I can still remember. Reminded of the boy who dug his pen nib into my leg long ago in a Peterborough infant school classroom, I am shocked by this sudden act of spite. It leaves me speechless. I do not want to hold her hand and walk with her, I feel outraged still and want to hurt her back, but the prefect prevents me. We are given money for the collection and marched in the crocodile along the back lanes and country roads until we come to the church. Inside it's freezing and the sermon goes on interminably.

Later, other girls tell me about the organist, whose hobby it is to show girls the belfry by ushering them up the ladder to the belfry and peering up their skirts as they climb up. Girls in the know always insist that he go first, they tell me. It makes sense, but I don't understand this sexual fascination; I don't even understand it is sexual, and just have to take it on trust that some men like to look at lisle stockings and navy blue knickers from below. Why they do remains a mystery.

At twelve I am a daydreamer, the daughter with the glasses and the plate to push back the protruding teeth, the curly, unfashionable hair. Knobbly kneed and elbows jabbing things off shelves all around.

"Sorry!"

"Why can't you be more careful?" My body is growing too fast. I don't know what each bit is doing. I fall, stumble, drop things, upset people and objects, lose my temper, throw things and miss, am unattractive to the point of being ugly. Janet is growing even faster, her long, thin legs bending in strange directions when photographed, her face a freckle holding big tombstone teeth, ginger hair bouncing around her head. She's bigger than I am now. She still hasn't forgiven my father. What for, she doesn't say, but he has tried every way he knows to please her. In Janet's bedroom sits a sad teddy bear, forehead scarred and burnt from the fire she let him fall on. Only this way, scarred and damaged, is he loveable. Our father made him, out of a kit he bought, each bit separately sewn and stuffed, eyes inserted, mouth and nose applied. When he gave Bear to her, she wouldn't look at him, wouldn't hold or play with him, didn't thank our father for the gift, though our mother tried to coax her.

Father was disappointed; he had taken a pride in the bear and his skill in making it and needed some recognition. Bear sat, neglected in her room until he fell onto the small two-bar electric fire in her bedroom, where she shut herself away in the evenings, and was horribly burned. She can feel sorry for him now, and so can endure his company. All her relationships are like this; the need for control is so powerful.

We still fight. I find school friendships difficult, but take pride in what I can do well, which at the moment is writing poetry. I am religious at twelve, filled with moral high purpose and stunned by the hypocrisy of the world. I write my poems in a secret book, decorate the pages with ornate flowers and into the book go all my secret thoughts, religious idealistic dreaming, private experiences.

Christmas, and the family are together in the same room, with my uncle and aunt, trying to be jolly. There is an uneasy truce between my parents at Christmas. When my father dares to risk some of his worse jokes, my aunt says "Oh really, Arthur," in a *tut-tut, naughty boy* tone of voice, but laughs, as does my father, delighted to have an audience. My uncle is also an engineer, a far more successful one than my father, and is already quite rich. He buys, sells and hires out heavy plant and has a well-kept works in Lowestoft. The two men have something in common and my father enjoys my uncle's company very much. He has no male friends since we left Peterborough. My uncle, a gentle jovial giant, loves the company of children and is delighted when he makes them laugh. He is my hero, ever since he bought us a proper ship's rope ladder to climb trees with, and a huge black rubber inner tube, from a tractor or plane, on which we could bounce for hours. My father cannot compete with this at all. He has no idea about what we like and never asks us, choosing instead to give us presents that he thinks we should like and which he considers to be bargains. My uncle sits, watching us. My cousin, a smaller version of his father, is curled up beside him, comfortable with everything. My aunt is chatting to my mother about a family visit the next day and what they should take. My father senses a lull in the conversation.

The big sofa sags under the weight of them. They are all laughing. I am looking at one of my presents, a crystal growing kit, wondering how soon I can start to use it.

Suddenly my father jumps up and goes out of the room. A few moments later he is back again, with something in his hand. I am not paying attention, have no idea how I am to be humiliated.

"Look at this," says my father. "Caroline writes these." He is smiling with the pride of one who has a secret trophy to reveal. The book is open, the contents exposed, my uncle invited to inspect these, my most intimate thoughts. I feel myself go cold inside, then red-hot. He knows my secret hiding place! He has been into my room. What else does he know about me? The answer, I know now, is 'nothing'. He isn't interested in me at all, only in showing me off to someone he wants to impress.

I fly towards them, seize the book with both hands; tug it away, tearing it. Fury overwhelms me. My mother says nothing; does nothing. She is interested in my rebelliousness, though. Maybe it gives her some clues about fighting back.

My uncle looks at me with concern.

"Caroline. I didn't know it was private. I'm sure your father didn't mean …"

"It's private. He never asked. It's private. You can't go and take people's private things and show them to everyone." The book is under my arm. I am very angry. Also, I want to cry. My father tries clumsily to smooth it over.

"It's only a book, nothing to get so upset about." He is sniggering. I hate him.

I scream: "It's a private book. You have no right to look at my private things." And I storm out. The book is ruined now for me. It has been violated. It will never be read again calmly with enjoyment. The memory spoils it, totally. I write on bits of paper and hide them away instead. This secrecy eventually proves my undoing.

At twenty-two, I have a biscuit tin full of poems hidden under the eaves of the room in Wandsworth I share with Steven. We have an old four-poster bed, a couple of sticky, inelegant chests of drawers and a washing basket in our room. I paint him asleep in the bed and realise I love him. He does not interfere with my writing at all. He's really a jazz man, and dislikes the male poets he knows, but he encourages me to write and perform. He does not invade my space and he respects my privacy. The biscuit tin still stays hidden. I raid it now and then and take pieces away to read at college.

When we have to move, because the landlord has decided to sell up, the biscuit tin remains behind, as we ferry stuff out to the Ford Popular and make the trip to Battersea to our new accommodation. By the time I remember it, it's too late; other people have moved in and the flat is as clean as a whistle.

A summer day, and my father has an interview at a local engineering plant. He is expected to wear a suit but can't find the tie, cuff links and socks he wants to wear with it. The suit is old and greasy, though my mother has tried to sponge and press it.

My father bellows down the stairs to the wife who will hear only a muffled roar in the back of her ears like the distant boom of the sea.

"Edith! What have you done with my tie?" She looks at us, puzzled, trying to decipher the message.

"What does he want?"

"He wants his tie."

She calls up to him, "It's in the back of the drawer." Then to us, "I told him where it was. He doesn't listen."

"Edith!" More bellowing. She rises wearily and goes upstairs. Janet and I look at one another. We will never allow a man to summon us like a slave, we think.

He needs to be babied, attended to, paid attention to. We get in the way most of the time.

When I am fourteen, I get a puppy. It's an uncontrolled boxer dog pup, a free spirit if there ever was one, whose delight in life and the doggy pursuits of chasing rabbits and squirrels and fighting other bigger dogs endear him to me greatly. His name is Nero.

My father is in a temper again. He's in the room referred to as *Father's pig sty*, and he's lost some papers. It's not surprising as there are papers everywhere in his room. He stamps around blaming some mysterious powers that have caused his papers to be lost. My mother is no help. He stamps through into the kitchen and searches the dresser, knocking things over as he goes.

"Where the hell is the bloody thing?" he asks. "Have you seen it, Edith?" But she hasn't, and she's tired of his tantrums.

"You've probably put it down somewhere," she says with a cool lack of interest. This infuriates him even more. Just then, Nero, my boxer puppy, bounds into the room, jumping round the table legs and barking at the commotion. My father goes to kick him. I've had enough, enough of the bullying and the shouting. Nero is a puppy and my father is hitting him. I go to the kitchen drawer and get out a knife.

"Leave him alone! He's a puppy; he hasn't seen your blessed papers. Don't you dare kick him again." I stand close to my father. I hold the knife up. I am still a great deal smaller than he, but I am very determined. He mutters something and goes out. My mother, as usual, appears indifferent.

When things are going well, which is not often, he's better company, but these days he's very depressed and unable to communicate with anybody. My mother senses he's depressed but does not know what to do about it. The family withdraw from him more and more. He is unable to make real contacts and begins to live in his own world, where music is the only thing that brings comfort.

My mother, meanwhile, does the best she can. She doesn't work and has no distractions from the house and the dreary existence of tending to her family's needs. Her own needs, whatever they are, are largely unmet. Gradually the distance and the hatred grow between my mother, brother and sister and my father. I stay in between, trying to gain what I need from them both, but it is heavy going.

School provides further occasions for humiliation and awkwardness with the advent of Greek dancing. Lumpen fourteen- and fifteen-year-olds, dressed in flimsy Greek tunics, are obliged to perform Isadora Duncan-inspired dances, which involve a great deal of waving the arms around in a vague fashion and Greek poses on one leg with the other lifted and bent, and dancing in a circle. Girls not really in charge of their own growing bodies cavort and clomp their way around the gym twice a week, trying to look graceful.

Miss Serjeant, the dancing teacher, was a horse-faced battleaxe who never smiled or looked at you, but devoted all her energy to moving bodies about. Suddenly, when you were preparing to position yourself, she would stride up behind you and wrench an arm backwards, or shove a foot into a different position. It never failed to startle. When this did not turn us into swan-like creatures, graceful and calm, country dancing was introduced which was much more fun. *Strip the Willow* and maypole-dancing were now listed among our accomplishments. Once, *The Lancers* was tried, as an experiment, with disastrous results. I remember being completely disabled by laughter as girls fell over, collided, lost their way and collapsed, hysterical with mirth. Miss Serjeant was not amused. Later we were obliged to learn ballroom dancing, which was less funny and slightly easier, as we could all just about manage the one two-three, one-two-three, steps of the waltz, to the tune of *Tammy*. I was always put as the lead, which has given me problems when dancing ever since. At school, we were all bright enough to realise that school dances, soon to be started with a boys' school nearby, would involve the ballroom dances we had learned, and we did our best to go through the motions.

I am thirteen and in love with my cousin, shamelessly pursuing him and his friends whenever we met. In our holidays in Lowestoft with my aunt and uncle, my cousin lets us come with him on his adventures. We cycle with him and a friend to a gravel pit and look for fossils. My cousin has a huge ammonite he found there, pearly and gorgeous, some pyrites and a bone from a dinosaur's vertebra.

We find smaller, but equally interesting fossils and minerals, and the excitement we feel is enormous. We search the beaches for agates, cornelians and pieces of amber, tumbled and wave tossed, which glow amid the pebbles as we scour the shingle banks, walking towards the light and looking always for the toffee light that glows through the small, wonderfully striped and coloured stones.

We take small bags with us and walk with bare, tender feet along the shingle banks of Pakefield beach, inhaling the fresh salty smell of the tide as it slurrs up against the shingle bank and rolls away again, tumbling the pebbles steeply down into the sliding froth of foam. The dry shingle is more difficult to explore. Beach coating gives each pebble a salty film, which we lick off if the pebble is transparent. These are the larger stones and finding an agate amongst them is more difficult but more rewarding when it happens. A beautiful translucent pink and orange pebble reveals itself to me when a shower of rain dampens the shingle beach I am resting on. Moving my arm back and forth to sweep new layers of stones reveals more, as the deeper we go the damper the stones become. Every so often we pause for one of Tweed's ice creams, when the van stops at the cliff top. The smell of ice cream on a hot, sandy beach is still one of my favourite smells.

If our cousin gets tired of these activities, he has the grace not to say so.

I still have a bagful of semiprecious pebbles I collected as a child, now polished and smooth, and can remember where I found each one.

Later, we camped with our own children at Southwold for several summers and let them explore the beach. I told my youngest son, then aged about five, that I had looked for semiprecious pebbles on this beach, when I was a child; ones that the light shone through and were reddish brown, or cream.

"Like this one?" he asked innocently, picking up a perfect golden-brown agate, striped with darker bands, and handing it to me. I held it up and admired it.

"I don't believe it! You just picked up a perfect specimen! How dare you, when I've been looking for ages!" Collapsing in giggles, he went off highly elated to continue the task I had begun thirty years before.

I learned a poem in school, by Eleanor Farjeon:

'Once as I wandered free from care
In happy days of sun and air
I chanced upon a little cove
Where all the sand was treasure trove
And all the pebbles in the sea
Were jasper or chalcedony...'

I longed to find this beach, with its treasure trove of stones: jasper, agate, quartz, jet, cornelian, citrine, bloodstone, chalcedony, serpentine, and I found occasional pebbles wherever I looked, on beaches in Cornwall, Dorset, East Anglia, Scotland, Morocco, Turkey. It remains a passion.

The North Sea, cold and rough as it is, was a constant challenge to us as children, once we had learned to swim. We plunged in, all goose pimples and white skinny arms, in our ruched bathing costumes, gasping as the first wave smacked against our belly buttons. My aunt would watch anxiously from the beach, ready with towels and admiration. Once, when Janet and I were up to our bottoms in the cold sea, a larger than average wave loomed over us, menacingly. We tried to run for the shore but the stones slipped and rolled under our feet. Crash! The water came down on top of us, rolling us both upside down and knocking us like skittles. Somehow we emerged, howling, and stumbling, from the water, blood dripping down our legs where the wave had pushed us down and dragged us along the gravel. I realise now how lucky we were to have got off so lightly. The steeply shelving beach was, in fact, quite dangerous for children to swim from, and the next year a policeman drowned there, trying to rescue a child. The child reached shore; the policeman had a heart attack and drowned.

At the top of the cliffs where my aunt and uncle lived was a grassy area sprinkled with hawthorn trees and daisies and clumps of alexanders, which looked a bit like celery but had a strange smell. We referred to this land as The Acre, and there were mobile homes dotted over it, but few people to be seen, and it was the perfect place to play hide and seek, or spy on the lovers. Later, our second son fell in love with a girl whose parents started their married life in a mobile home on The Acre, one of the strange intertwining coincidental things in our lives.

Pakefield was in many ways a delightful place for children to holiday in. It was near Lowestoft, but without the crowds. The beach shone like a beacon at the end of the path opposite my aunt and uncle's house, the intensity of the light grew as one approached, and then would come the sandy run down through the gap in the cliff top, the sinking into soft sand with exhausted legs, reaching damper and firmer sand embedded with shells, then the shingle bars interspersed with wet, sandy strips and the weed, driftwood and empty crab shells at the tide line, then the water, approaching and retreating. We never tired of it, though my cousin must have been extremely bored, trailing behind two little girls who only wanted to go beach combing.

There was a darker side to life here: the wolves that lived in the enclosure where the electricity substation was. This enclosure was in between two houses and we had to pass it on our way to the bread shop, where our aunt had a daily order of crusty rolls to be collected when we stayed. We would go along the road skipping as children do, then our footsteps would slow as we reached the dark, overgrown enclosure of the substation. Faint noises came from the site. Janet grew pale. My cousin said, "Wolves." Ninety percent of me knew there could be no wolves there, the other ten percent wasn't so sure.

"Let's run past." The shadowy wolves with their invisible ravenous jaws and intelligent eyes slunk under the dark trees, but they never attacked. My sister was terrified of them. At night we could hear the train into Lowestoft huffing its way down the line. Memories of *The Three Little Pigs* and the huffing and puffing wolf were strong in both our minds.

"Wolves," Janet whispered. Cruelly I did not disagree, even though I knew it was the train. Traditional children's stories are full of references to wolves; they are knowing, cruel and hungry. Everywhere the Big Bad Wolf beckons little children and gobbles them up, even if they have woodcutter fathers to protect them. The fear is always present. Only an encounter with a real wolf dissolves the fear; at least I thought that was the case until our mother took us to the zoo at Whipsnade. We walked past the wolves' enclosure and the wolves, looking bored, trotted about under the trees. Their eyes were fearless. These were good dogs turned into bad predators, lupine, voracious, savage. But they didn't look it. As we were leaving the zoo, a terrible sound arose from the enclosure. The wolves were howling. Every hair on my neck bristled. Janet, whose fears about wolves had begun to diminish at the sight of these dog-like creatures, froze to the spot.

"They just want their dinner," my mother said. "They're hungry."

"Do they ever get out?" we wanted to know.

"No, they're kept inside that fence there—can you see?"

Later, I mused on this fear of wolves. We liked dogs. We played with them, trusted them to bark at intruders, enjoyed throwing sticks for them and watching them romp and roll over. What if they showed a darker side? What if the dog next door suddenly discovered the wolf inside herself and became savage, attacking us? The dual nature of things was troubling. Good dog or bad dog? Friend or enemy? The howl had made the difference; it instilled a fear into us that the sight of them had not induced. Later I learned that place names in England starting with the word 'Ull' describe the sound of a wolf's howl and that the word itself means wolf. We were not frightened of much, but for my sister wolves were always the terror, while for me lions, which I had seen ripping their bloody dinners to shreds and roaring, were much more threatening. My dreams were haunted by lions appearing on the landing, in the garden, escaped from a zoo or circus, more mean and ruthless in their pursuit of quarry than the wolves could ever be. The sheer physical power and smell of them was what I feared. Wolves were shadowy, insubstantial creatures in comparison.

If my cousin had any such fears, he never told us about them. Practical, and surrounded by the love, attention and security of his parents, he got on with the business of living with cheerful efficiency.

Fishing was an activity my cousin was keen on then. With his father's help in organising rod, lines bait and light, he went on to the beach at night with a sea rod and let us join him. Hunched up and cold on the crunching shingle of the beach, we watched the stars and waited, happy to be with him. Perhaps we put him off, for he never caught anything on these trips while we were with him. He took us to the Broads on our bikes instead and made us bait our own hooks with live maggots. He caught perch, but disliked catching eels, which were numerous there, as they fouled up the lines and were hard to manage if you did get them ashore. We went out in a rowing boat and fished, finding a coypu dead on the towpath and marvelling at its huge yellow-orange teeth. This secret world of boys was fascinating to me. I much preferred it to anything else on offer in what was then termed girls' interests. Why didn't girls go fishing? Why didn't girls explore, climb dangerous cliffs or go on long treks across country? Would I be condemned to cook meals, sew clothes and clean instead for the rest of my life? I quite liked to cook and sew, but that was not the point. I studied the Famous Five books, hoping for some guidance, but all the characters seemed flawed to me. Who wanted to be like George, impossibly butch and sneering at the hapless Anne? Who wanted to be Anne, forever clearing up, tending wounds and making meals? Not me.

I had abandoned dolls very young, finding my cousin's meccano set much more interesting; his wind-up Hornby train a delight. At home I built tiny gardens in trays, invented imaginative games where Janet and I could dress up and play pirates, gypsies and bandit queens, and made contraptions for looking into birds' nests without disturbing the occupants. Janet and I had been separated forever by her separations from our mother and me, and time spent away from the family home. She seemed to live in a world where to be silent and on the verge of tears brought her an audience unavailable to me. No one wanted to see those beautiful brown eyes fill up with tears, least of all our mother, who felt guilty at having been parted from her though it was hardly her fault. I loved our mother, but I couldn't cling to her. Maybe the fact of being left in the family home while she was ill made the separations easier for me, maybe I was in any case more bonded with my father, flawed though that was; maybe I was anyway more robust and rebellious by nature than my sister. As time went by and we grew older, I began to realise that vulnerability as a manipulative tool for getting your own way did not serve any useful purpose, neither did my strident demands for attention. The survival strategies we employed as children took us a long way into our adult lives. Only when I found someone able to say, over and over again, "I'm not going anywhere," whenever the urge to rampage came upon me, did I learn that my whole modus operandi had been based on shouting at a deaf mother who sometimes wasn't there, and when she was there, might as well not have been at times when she couldn't hear me. Janet's partners had inconstancy built in, and this was reinforced by my mother's subtle discouragement of any that might have been suitable.

Janet ignores my father, or fights against him. There are no times when a better, more positive relationship is possible, because she won't allow it and he doesn't know how. Men for my sister are problematic.

Puberty hit us both hard when it arrived. I had to get used to a body that was not the tidy, trim little girl's body that had served me so well for so long. Instead it became a place of secret shame, with smells and excretions that disgusted me.

At fourteen, my body was developing in a normal if haphazard way and I had prominent breasts, a little lop sided, but I guessed they'd grow. My mother had ducked out of explaining the mysteries of menstruation to me until her hand was forced and I was very ignorant, as indeed my mother was. She still advocated old-fashioned Kotex or Dr White's pads and a belt, which were uncomfortable and bulky, and in vain I had to read discarded Tampax instructions hoping for a clue to the mystery I knew other girls had solved. I believe my mother understood that we were growing up and hid from it, as it brought closer the eventual day when we would leave her alone with my father. My sister decided that she would not grow up and publicly declared this, sucking her thumb until she was seventeen, and curling up in a foetal position on the couch. Amy, our friend from the next village, was very different, although she was physically small, and wore hooped paper petticoats that stuck out in a circle behind her when she bent over, and patent leather shoes, in which, it was said, boys could see the reflection of your knickers. She was feminine and had a mother who liked to dress up and who encouraged her daughter to take a pride in her appearance.

Meanwhile, here was I, nearly fifteen and I still hadn't got a bra. At school I was the butt of many jokes, and I resorted to standing unnaturally straight hoping my average sized breasts wouldn't show. Finally I challenged our mother about it, and after quite a struggle she agreed to let me have a bra. The struggle was the same for deodorant, tampons, tights, shoes and hairstyles. She did not want us to be women and gave us no encouragement at all. She was, I think, frightened of our sexuality and also afraid it might lead us away from her. Until we were earning we could not afford these things for ourselves, and it was unpleasant having to insist she buy them for us. Our father would occasionally comment on how we looked, mostly favourably, and Janet always scowled while I accepted the comments for what they were. We were growing up, whether Janet wanted to or not. We began going out to local dances and carefully vetted parties and inexorably moved more and more away from the circle of home. Our mother tolerated it. She had no choice. Our brother however, never had the same opportunity. His world was school and home, at my mother's side, and he would not leave her. As he grew, he and my father became rivals, and my mother clung more and more to my brother. Oedipus was born again.

Without an effective peer group or partner to lead him away from her, he remained trapped with her until she died.

It's May, and I am fourteen. I have cycled back from school to Somersets, the four and a half miles taking me longer than it should because as always I dawdle and take my time. I stop by the canal bridge, to watch the swans that are nesting there. I stop by the stream to see if the kingfisher has nested in the clay bank as he does most years. When I arrive home, the house is as it always is. My brother who has come home from his school earlier is in his bedroom. My sister, who cycled back ahead of me, has gone out again to look at the pigs farrowing in the field. My dog greets me with frenzied tail wagging and licks. I have to take him out later. My mother is in the kitchen, looking worried in front of a cookery book.

"Hello, Caroline. What shall I get everyone for supper? I don't know, sometimes I feel like just like clearing off and leaving you to it." This is nothing new, she's often at her wits' end to find us food that we can eat and she can afford. She continues her monologue. "I can give Janet a Vesta Curry. Father won't eat that, of course." Here she sighs loudly. "You'll eat fish, won't you?"

"Yes, Mum, I'll eat anything."

"I don't know if Douglas will eat fish. It is difficult finding something you'll all eat." Finally she settles on fish pie, with boiled carrots and peas. "Douglas won't eat carrots. You don't mind carrots, do you?"

"No, Mum. Can I help?"

"You can lay the table. If you get married, don't ever let your children get fussy about their food." I think to myself that from what I can see of marriage, the whole arrangement would have to be very different if I were to even consider it.

I lay the table and help her get the food ready. My father has come in from wherever he has been and gone out again without telling anyone where he is going.

I call up the stairs to Douglas and go outside to find Janet, who is by the pig field, watching the new piglets squirming against their mother as they batter her teats with their snouts.

"Dinner's ready!" She comes in slowly. Douglas appears, his small, pale face streaked with grubby marks. We wash our hands and sit down. There is no sign of our father. Annoyed that he is missing, she chides him in his absence.

"Where is Father? He knows what time it is. Just like him to go off when the meal's ready. Caroline, go and put this in the oven. It'll be ruined." She looks ready to cry. Clearly it has been a bad day. We eat glumly. Father comes in halfway through and Mum has to get up again to fetch his food. He expects her to, but if she once were to ask him to fetch it himself, he would say he wasn't hungry and that he'd eat it later.

She fetches it and he sits down. She glances at the expression on his face as he eats it. He pulls a face.

"What's the matter? Don't say you don't like fish, please." She says this in a beseeching way, a sob in her voice. He takes no notice. "I took such trouble ..."

"Fish always reminds me of my prep school, stinks the house out."

"Oh dear. You like fish, don't you, Caroline?" She wants support anywhere she can find it.

"Of course I like fish. This is very nice." My father is searching round in his stock of anecdotes and memories to find something amusing to say about the supper.

"Always repeats on me, fish." He can't stop himself. Douglas is eating a minute portion of fish and peas, but no carrots; Janet has eaten her Vesta Curry; our mother is trying to feed herself but isn't enjoying the meal. Father makes a pronouncement.

"Going over to Frimley tonight." Mother looks at him. She hasn't heard him.

"What?" She turns her aid up.

"I said I'm going over to Frimley tonight."

"Oh yes?" She waits to see if more will follow.

"Going to see Tony about the organ." She is concentrating. He says it again, more loudly.

"I heard what you said." But she doesn't know how to respond to him. He stands up, leaving half the fish pie on his plate. She looks rejected and upset again.

It's like this every mealtime, just about, except when we have visitors, when he talks with a false bonhomie and makes subtle digs about our mother, highlighting her deafness. They have nothing in common to talk about except for the birdlife in the garden. She isn't interested in his music, or old Tony's organ, or the Lodge, or the folk club, or anything he is involved in. He can't remember what her interests are now.

After supper I take my dog for a walk. He, at least, presents an uncomplicated view of the world. My father says that if he can't fight it, mate with it or eat it, his solution is to pee on it. He's right, but the joke is so worn by now it no longer makes me smile. He has never ever taken our dog for a walk. He has only once taken us out for one. Other people's fathers do things with them, I realise, but ours never does.

He has occasional flashes of interest when our lives tally with his in some way. He buys a steam engine for Douglas one Christmas and makes it work while Douglas has to sit by and watch his father playing with it. Douglas puts the steam engine away and never gets it out again.

Our lives are reaching outside the home, and we become aware that there are amusements of which he would disapprove, mostly rock and roll. He plays his music to me—Mahler, Berlioz, Mozart— and the tango music he bought as a boy in the South of France, and I listen to these knowing that if that's all he can give me, then I'll take what I can from that. He will not pay for us to have music lessons, but he subscribes to a music magazine which he expects me to read, and takes me to the Festival Hall from time to time with my uncle, to hear his favourite works performed.

But other music is beginning to filter through into my life.

In the world outside Somersets, Elvis, Little Richard and Jerry Lee Lewis were setting music halls and cinemas alight with the energy of young, rebellious, passionate sex. No matter that Little Richard became a Seventh Day Adventist and was gay, no matter that Jerry Lee had a child bride, no matter that Elvis became what he became, for us they were heroes and they shook up and evicted the crooners and the squeaky clean girl singers with their perms and pointed bras and gave us something altogether more to our liking. We were getting restless. Janet bought Cliff Richards' *Livin' Doll*, I bought Johnny Cash's *Big River*; we clubbed together to buy Buddy Holly, Bobbie Darrin, Neil Sedaka and Adam Faith.

Janet and I began to investigate the possibilities of our village and the town beyond. Finally we found a traditional jazz venue in Camberley, which attracted Sandhurst cadets. This was a drawback, as they appeared to have no chins and to wear cravats and cavalry twills, while the Aldershot squaddies who went there to fight them wore a suit jacket and a tight pair of jeans, with winklepickers and a great deal of grease disguising their army haircuts. The third group of people frequenting this venue were the jazz freaks, identified by their long hair, beards, sandals and black sweaters. It was sub-Beat costume, and they said 'man' a lot and smoked Gauloise or Camel cigarettes. I found this group more attractive than the other two, as there was a certain amount of anarchy involved in their appearance and lifestyle, and they treated women with an openness that was refreshing. There were brief, intense exchanges between members of this group, about poetry, jazz, Soho nightlife, dreams, politics, literature. They frequented Ken Collyer's club when they had money, but came to Camberley to stomp and beat time to Ottilie Patterson and Chris Barber's *Green Onions*, and *Tiger Rag*. Usually there was a local band playing cover versions of traditional numbers. Jazz bands in the South of England at that time were ten a penny, while the rare appearances of black American jazz musicians created a fever among anyone professing to like jazz. Those who were really hip listened to 'Bird' Parker, Mingus, or Monk, making do in their absence with Dick

Morrisey, Phil Seaman and other homegrown heroes. Camberley was not so advanced.

Good music to stomp to was what we wanted; its pedigree was unimportant.

It was around this time that Wendlesham Hall began to arrange dances with a neighbouring boys' public school. So starved were we of male company that we went out of our way to make ourselves look attractive, even for these acne-speckled fifteen-year-olds. Sandra spent hours combing her hair up into a beehive, Valerie slapped pancake on her rather grey skin and ringed her eyes with mascara until Miss Maude made her wash it off, saying it looked cheap, while I desperately looked for something — anything — to wear that would make me look feminine and attractive. I failed, but the boy I spent the evening with was so glad to find a listening ear and a sympathetic presence, coming as he did from a home and school that encouraged neither, that we got on very well. I was to find this more and more as I got to know boys my own age. Often they were uncritical of me and anxious to talk about themselves, so that a rather one-sided friendship was possible. I had had years of practice at listening to my father, after all. What I had had no practice in was talking about myself to someone wanting to hear. I was entrusted with some important confidences by the young males I knew; about boarding school life, abuse, and failed relationships. I was good at listening to others, but I had not yet found anyone who was able to listen to me.

There was Duncan who told me about a recurring dream he had in which he woke in the night to find the house on fire. He knew that if could turn on the tap in the washbasin and flood the house the fire would be extinguished, so he set off across the room towards the tap, but in his dream his feet were sticking to the floor and the floor itself was tilting upwards into a steep slope. He clawed his way up this steep slope, while smoke and flames licked at his ankles. He reached the tap, turned it on — and blood came out in a bright red stream.

This nauseating dream made a deep impression on me, but I learned later he was one of the first of our generation to have experimented with narcotics and I wonder now if his dream derived from his fear and longing for a heroin hit.

James wanted my advice on what to tell his younger brother about the school he was due to attend. His younger brother was gentle and quiet, and as James spoke, I could understand what he was worried about. Bullying, beatings, and sexual abuse went on in the English public school system then and now. As a leading politician said when asked about it: *'My dear, I was buggered at public school, everyone is, it's part of school life.'* At fifteen and sixteen my understanding of it was nil, but I could sense the distress and pain of my friend.

Only when Sam came into my life when I was nineteen did I find someone trustworthy enough to tell my deepest secrets to. Though we didn't stay together, as our paths took us in opposite directions geographically, we both subsequently worked in occupations where listening was a crucial component.

THIRTEEN

I found girls of my own age hard work. Trudi, Tricia and Maureen formed the basis of a girls' gang to which all aspired to join, but were excluded from by being inferior in some way. My glasses and curly hair debarred me from their circle. Sneering, laughing behind their hands and making snide remarks, Trudi, Tricia and Maureen made the lives of many girls miserable. The in-crowd and its disciples constituted the majority of my year. True, there were some who were not obsessed with boys, fashion and makeup, but unless they had money, powerful parents or great beauty, they were regarded as losers. I couldn't compete and anyway, did not especially want to, or so I told myself. Anyway, bringing people home was embarrassing. My father's odd behaviour and my mother's deafness were things that had to be explained to new visitors, and our lack of money showed. Much as I admired music boxes with twirling ballerinas on the top, or model Coronation coaches, or face powder compacts with pictures of swans, or fashionable clothes, I knew our family couldn't afford such things and I told myself I didn't need them anyway. Close relationships with other girls brought out the insecure and jealous side of my nature. This was easily triggered by them finding a boyfriend, or preferring the company of another girl, and would result in a sudden and unexplained switch in their allegiance, which would leave me depressed for weeks. I grew to realise how teenaged girls could humiliate the males around them as well as one another, and that this was something I could share with the boys I knew.

I wouldn't, and didn't, play these spiteful games. Too much of that was already going on at school and at home around me. I needed straightforward communications with people and insisted on them, though this was difficult for them at times. It took me a long time to find a group of women that I could feel safe with, and who would let me be myself.

What I had, I was beginning to realise, was a brain that worked quite well, and an interest in literature, philosophy, politics and social issues that gave me some common ground with a few adults I knew. Perhaps there was an escape from this hellish place called adolescence, after all. When Trudi, Tricia and Maureen and some of their cohorts were finally expelled for leaving the premises after dark and going to parties in town, I missed their glamorous presence, but felt, at the same time, a sense of relief. Those of us left behind developed our own styles more confidently in the knowledge that we would not be under the sneering scrutiny of the group again.

We are staying with our cousin in Lowestoft. He has been at boarding school and has learned hundreds of rugby songs, which he sings snatches of to us whenever his mother isn't listening. We are all ears, but he misses out the really rude bits of *The Good Ship Venus* and *Four and Twenty Virgins*, and we have to fill in the gaps. We plead with him to tell us the missing words, but he has chivalrous ideas about what isn't suitable for our ladylike ears. He is prepared to take us to the concert in the pier ballroom, however, and as he's very tall for his age and our aunt feels he'll protect us, we are allowed to go along. I am wearing a home-sewn dress, green with some pattern on it that I sent off for in *Women's Own*. I have my hair up in a French pleat, which won't stay up, but I backcomb it frantically to add height. Our mother has no idea about fashion or what we should be wearing, so I have resorted to making my own clothes, which have strange hems and bits of cotton hanging off them. I have only just mastered zip fasteners, and most of my dresses have lopsided zips, so that the material puckers unpleasantly and the zip end digs into my neck. Later I discover a halter neck style, which needs no zip, but is gathered with a cord around the neck. Janet tends to wear the one or two nice dresses she has acquired, which are tasteful but not in any way exciting. I am not, for once, jealous of her. She is tongue-tied with most men, aloof to the point of rudeness with anyone she doesn't know well. Is it shyness, or fear? I have given up trying to find out. She never smiles, while I enjoy myself. We have brought along some summer frocks in candy stripes, which our mother has bought from C & A in London, on a rare shopping trip, but we feel they are a bit ordinary for a night on the prom. We put on black eyeliner and pale pink lipstick, which shocks our aunt slightly.

The promenade is buzzing with Lowestoft young walking to the pier and my eyes are popping out of my head. There are some fisher boys just back from sea, dressed in the most amazing suits I have ever seen; pink with a black bootlace tie, black brocade with fancy waistcoats, suede brothel creepers, lime green socks. I am amazed and my cousin has to call me away for fear they take offence. Fluorescent socks are the rage and the local boys are wearing pink, green and yellow ones with their crepe-soled shoes. They have slicked back hair and a quiff with what we learn is a duck's arse at the back. The fisher boys, who have the money in this town, make their own fashion and scorn to be labelled as anything other than what they are. Leading hard lives, drinking hard, fighting hard, they bear the marks of the hawsers, ropes and cables that have sheared off a finger here, scarred a cheek, trapped a foot there. The fights leave their marks too; you can't be dragged across a coal depot face down by your feet and not have wounds to show; dark-red, weeping grazes filled with coal grit.

Their formidable scars and hard faces contrast oddly with their gorgeous attire; these are men who know how to live, and how to die. They dominate the dance floor on the pier, and Janet and I can only watch from the balcony the seething mass of dancers as it undulates, spins and bobs. The band is mainly playing cover versions of Eddie Cochran, Little Richard, the Big Bopper, Buddy Holly. Some local youths, friends of my cousins, are persuaded to dance with us. My cousin will not dance; he is so tall, he attracts attention and he dislikes it. Quick! The last dance is here. We look round anxiously to see who will dance with us. Nobody does. A fight is going on, on the promenade; two of the fisher boys are swinging broken bottles at one another, while their girls hang on to their other arm. Our cousin steers us away from them, and we skirt neatly away across the clock golf course, past the little boating lake, now closed for the night, into the safety of the side streets.

Auntie has waited up for us, relieved that we have come to no harm. Uncle appears from somewhere and asks if we would like to have some chips. He makes them for us, taking his time, and we are nearly asleep when he brings them up. Our own father has never made food for us because we might like it; in fact, he hardly ever cooks now. Uncle goes out of his way to buy us treats; bags of crisp brown sweet-smelling fresh shrimps from the stall on the cliffs, which he sits and helps us peel, coconuts at Christmas, grapes and walnut whips for my mother. He has no ulterior motive; his own home was a poor one and now he's richer than we are he likes to please people by spoiling them a little. He and my aunt are happy together, and I learn how it is that people can live together in harmony, and that there are men who like the company of children and know how to make them smile. I learn and watch and later marry a man who also has this gift. This is certainly no accident.

My father, the engineer, has never had anyone think about what would please him. He has had no model of how a father might be. He has his own ideas about what he wants us to have, what he wants to give us, but there's no reference to us in any of this. The contrast between the two men is very marked, and my father feels it.

Born into a wealthy family, to a spoiled, nineteen-year-old beauty and a young army officer, my father arrived in the war-torn world of 1916. Being a large breech baby, his birth caused great pain to my grandmother, a fact she took no trouble to hide. His arrival interfered with her social life, and she was not ready to be anyone's mother. Although christened Constance Margaret, my grandmother was always known as Bill. My great-grandmother, a tiny formidable Welshwoman, took over my father's care. Bored, with my grandfather away, Bill began an affair with one of his subalterns that ended with my grandfather chasing them both down the street. My father was handed over to a series of nannies and housemaids who carted him around like an inconvenient package, dumping him where it suited them. He formed a very close attachment to Maggie, who was paid to mind him, but who went back to live in Yorkshire when my father was four. He cried when she left, at the loss of another part-mother that could not be really his. Not long after this, my grandmother began a relationship with a playboy villain, Basil Hamborough, who my father swears tried to kill him, thinking that by doing away with the son and heir, he could get his hands on my grandmother's money. He married my grandmother eventually and they went to live in the South of France, where my grandmother continued to live for much of her life. Basil left her once he realised the money was tied up in a convoluted trust and would never be his. My father was moved around the country during school holidays and sent to a prep school at the age of seven on the South Coast, where his father and new stepmother had settled. He explained this nomadic life he led by saying that the family were worried Basil would try and kidnap him. It is indisputable that his mother formed no close attachment to him as a baby, and that she was able to leave him with no evident qualms, referring to him as 'the brat'. His stepmother, already annoyed that Robbie, my grandfather, should have first married Bill, found her new little stepson, the son of her rival, difficult to handle, and was probably relieved when he went away to school. My grandfather did his best, but his attention was always divided between his new wife, his army postings and whatever chaos Bill was causing.

A mild-mannered, moderate man, who wiped the feet of his wife's Pekinese after their walk when he brought them home, and who had the air of someone perpetually in the wrong, my memory of him is of someone desperate to please, gentlemanly and with a keen but suppressed sense of mischief. His pranks as a young officer in a Yorkshire regiment were famous, from throwing a large green jelly over the balcony into the midst of the sedate dancers at the ballroom of the Scarborough hotel hired for the regimental ball, to using a tea tray to descend the staircase. His family had been shipbuilders on the Tyne at Gateshead, a long way removed from the Geeson clan who had terrorised the Borders with the Armstrongs in the Middle Ages, stealing sheep and conducting raids on their neighbours. Over the years, the Geeson clan had multiplied and gained respectability. My grandmother's father, also an army officer, died two years before my father was born, when my grandmother was seventeen, and I wonder if the death of her father, for this spoiled and beautiful only daughter, did not perhaps throw her rather too suddenly into the arms of my grandfather, another older military man.

The money that was settled on my grandparents on their marriage was held in a trust for my father, by the agreement of both sets of parents. This was in order to prevent Bill, known for her extravagance, from spending it all. I keep reminding myself that she was only eighteen when she married, nineteen when my father was born, yet it seems as though she had already been labelled by her own mother as immature and spendthrift. This family money was both a curse and a blessing. It gave my father some leverage with my mother, who had a small private income and was left the house by her Aunt Ethel. On the other hand, having the money as a backup, to be dished out at the discretion of the trustees, meant that he never had to think about finances when he took on some new venture. My mother worried about money all the time. There was never enough to go round, and she had never learned the skills of thrifty housekeeping. Neither did she work. My father tinkered with this and that, and always had enough money to pay for his own amusements, a staggering record collection and the latest gadget from the Argos catalogue.

My father embraced the new with enthusiasm, but also mended anything old that could still be of service. The garage was full of formica offcuts, pieces of ply, plumbing equipment, cable, wire, strips of veneer, boxes of brass sheet pieces, with tiny pieces cut out, gluepots, soldering equipment, tools for making fancy wooden joints, drain rods and chimney brushes. All were used and valued. If he had one real skill, it was in being able to mend and repair almost anything. What he did not have was any design flair at all, though he could be easily seduced into following the fashion of the day, which in the case of the kitchen, resulted in lots of speckled formica, mushroom paint and a cream Aga, with duck-egg tiles and a sink set into the work surface without a draining board, which as my mother pointed out was no use at all, as the water quickly collected around the rim on the work surface and warped the ply under the formica.

"He has no common sense," my mother would complain. "You

can't tell him anything." She was right; he never listened, to her or anybody. When the warped worktop became a real eyesore, shortly after he took over the washing up in an effort to wrest control from the family once again, he decided to install a new one, this time with a stainless steel draining board. It was a real climb down, and his displeasure was shown in the way he took over the whole kitchen for days in a very bad tempered way.

The kitchen is exactly as it was over forty years ago when he fitted it, and it has every design fault imaginable. The breakfast bar, very Fifties in concept, has a gap in it that is too narrow to admit anyone over a certain size. The fairy lights shaped like coronation coaches and bunches of grapes and lemons he tacked over the top and which are now removed, were too low and caught in your hair. The swing down counter top that fills in the gap is insecurely fastened and descends with a crash when you least expect it, and all the wall cupboard space is at a height where only he, at over six feet, could reach. To cap it all, the Aga is in a corner of the kitchen just behind the door leading to the rest of the house, so that anyone attempting to put anything into the oven, or take it out, is thrown forward onto their knees and forced to stick their head in the oven when anyone comes into the kitchen from the hall. Consequently, cooking is a rather dangerous activity, as there is no work space next to the Aga and one lives in fear of the door opening suddenly and smacking you in the back even when standing.

The family got used to this and approached the door from the hall with care when mealtimes came, as there was no other way into the dining room. There would have been another way in, through 'Father's pigsty,' but this was such an obstacle course that it was not to be attempted. Tackling it, you would need to edge past the three paste tables spread with sheet music and concertina parts, step over the expensive, fancy, electric sewing machine, shift the cabinet full of videos of French comedy actors, negotiate the overflowing filing cabinet, edge around the corner to where the serving hatch had once been, removing the broken chair awaiting repair, and then part the curtains to enter the dining room. There was punishment for those who attempted this route, as they would be shouted at if they disturbed anything, or even if they didn't.

We watched in amazement at times when a stranger who didn't

understand the rules of this house blithely broke the rules with the courage of the totally ignorant. They went into the pigsty, they commented (possibly) on the better use that could be made of the room, they agreed openly with my mother about the inconvenience of the Aga being where it was, they asked questions that no one dared to ask, with an innocence that was refreshing, such as 'Who has to do all the gardening?'— always a bone of contention, and 'It must be a bit awkward, having people come in through the kitchen if you're cooking.' Anyone doing this deliberately would then sit back and wait for the action to start. It was at times like these that my mother would decide she hadn't heard, unless she was sure the questioner was on her side.

The question of the garden was an interesting one. As the house and the extensive gardens around it were my mother's, but held in trust for my brother, my father felt he had no real stake in the property, though he spent a lot of time and money on the house over the years. The garden, which had been Ethel's pride and joy he had no interest in, and as years went by the brambles and weeds encroached more and more until the original garden was entirely lost under a sea of weeds. My brother, always the child in this household of battling adults and my mother's hostage, very rarely helped her in the garden, as she struggled to mow the lawns with a huge petrol driven mower and clear away some of the shoulder-high brambles. Neither did my sister help to any extent, and in her need to hoard filled up the garage, the porch, the old wash-house and her bedroom with junk. The garden became a battle ground between her and my father when she established a herb garden at a corner of the house. He pulled up the bay tree, saying it was undermining the foundations (true) and he then decided to build a patio around the house, digging up and destroying all her herbs as he progressed. Neither had spoken to the other about their plans.

Angry and upset, Janet spoke to me on the phone, ranting about this wanton destruction of her garden. Knowing things would never change, I challenged her to leave and get her own garden, her own place where she could do what she wanted with no interference. This wasn't what she wanted to hear, but she did it anyway.

She was then approaching forty and had never lived away from home. Thus I found myself in the position of mother, kicking my sister out of the nest, long after she should have flown. My mother never forgave me.

My sister's previous attempt to leave had involved her bravely finding accommodation in South London, and leaving it over the weekend while she went home, returning to find that her room had been slept in by someone else over the weekend and her rug damaged by cigarette burns. Incensed, she informed my mother, who told her not to stay there, but to return home at once. This she duly did and missed her opportunity to assert herself with her housemates, establish her independence and leave home for good.

I understood her situation too well.

I am twenty-one years old, and I have decided to be a teacher. Because I've worked for almost three years since leaving school, I'm eligible for a full grant, minus thirty pounds a year. My father refuses to pay me this, saying that as I'm female, I'll only get married and the training will be wasted. Finally I appeal and am awarded a full grant.

I attend a London college, for mature students, and meet Jacky, who is to become a lifelong friend. We decide to live together when we can find somewhere. I decide to find a bed-sitter for the time being, so that I can help her look.

The rooming house in Putney (which is how it is described) has an exotic mix of residents, all of them friendly, and my room is clean and comfortable, if small. Trains rattle past the back window every so often and shake the glass. The Belling cooker is tiny, the Ascot is ancient, but it's going to be home. I am delighted to have found it. I make friends with an elderly lady from Guyana who lives downstairs, and a Chinese prostitute on the first floor. I am a raw country girl, I have never lived in London and I am an innocent abroad, but I am learning fast. I am very pleased with myself.

Then my parents come up, bringing some of my belongings. Gingerly they approach the house and ascend the stairs to my bedroom on the second floor. My mother looks round.

"Oh, you can't live here!" she declares, distress in every syllable. "Oh, Caroline, you're not going to live here, are you?" All my excitement, all my enthusiasm drains away. But I am not going to give in. She narrows her eyes and looks around. I can see nothing wrong with it. She goes sulky quiet on me, martyred and silent.

"I am," I say, "until I can find a flat to share with Jacky. It will do for now; it's clean and cheap and very convenient." My father has been looking round thoughtfully. My mother realizes I'm not going to be put off. My father comments:

"I remember being in digs during the war. Do the trains bother you?"

I shake my head.

"You get used to them. Besides, I'm not in much." He smiles. This he understands. My mother sniffs again, disapprovingly. He isn't backing her up, as he should be doing. She might cry, later in the car. I hate her for having killed my achievement with her cold-water comments. She has done this once too often. Luckily I am strong and rebellious enough to know I need to survive away from her, away from all of them. Later she disapproves of other flats, houses, lodgers, neighbours, our poverty, (not so great, really), our decision to have a third child, our foster son, anything and everything that might hold me and keep me away from her and the environment she feels safe in.

Finally, years later, I have to write and tell her that her fears are not my fears, her life not my life, and that I cannot bear her anxieties as well as my own. Some support and encouragement is needed, I add, rather than this constant negative stuff. I say how much I value her as a mother, how much I've learned from her about being a good mother and the pleasure it gives me. I thank her for this. She sulks for weeks and I feel ungrateful and mean.

Leaving my own children at eighteen in dubious student flats for the first time, I am reminded of my own experience and strive not to perpetuate the same on them. I think I succeed, but probably fail in some other respect that they'll no doubt tell me about in due course.

My sister turns back at the first obstacle, her need for my mother's approval too strong to resist. *If you leave, I will never love you again.* My brother never even makes it past the front door.

I know where my mother's fears arise, understand how much of an orphan she still feels, how much she wants to recreate the home she lost when she was eight. My father will never be able to do this for her, although he, too, wants a home where he feels loved and wanted.

He gives her children; this he sees as his only achievement that is worth anything to her. They are doomed to be disappointed in one another and in us.

FOURTEEN

At school we are put under greater pressure, as O levels begin to loom. Also, I suspect that the school needs to attract more pupils and higher academic standards are being called for. Girls are now being expected to learn more of the sciences and apply a certain rigour to their learning. The Misses Potts, past their prime, are preparing to retire and are trying to make the most of the time they still have. We have a very odd assortment of teachers who join the school and vanish overnight after only a few months. There's Miss Froggett, a new geography teacher, whose hair is swept into an untidy chignon and whose bloated, red-flushed face sags as she falls asleep in front of the class. We do not know whether to be concerned, amazed, alarmed or relieved. She is arrested for being drunk and disorderly after falling down in the High Street during one Saturday afternoon. We do not see her again.

Miss Cathcart, six feet tall with the profile of an Egyptian pharaoh, all dyed black hair and ruby lipstick, takes us for maths. Her size and manlike figure contrast oddly with her voice, which is high, monotonous and droning, though decidedly female. She never laughs, never shouts, and never allows her voice to rise or fall with exasperation or excitement. I hate her, for no very good reason. Long division, multiplication of double figures, percentages, decimal points, all elude me. I can't grasp them. Yet at times, when I am posed a difficult problem, I can almost instantly come up with the right answer, without having any idea how I arrived at it. Naturally I am suspected of cheating. *Show your work!* is the exasperated comment at the side of yet another sum.

Hilary, a classmate whom I regard as stupid, is asked to explain long division to me. She has Miss Cathcart's total lack of imagination and spontaneity and refuses to allow me to try an inspired guess.

The discipline of having to follow a formula I did not understand to do a sum I could see in my head would probably have been good for me, if only I had been able to avoid the humiliation of ignorance. I knew I was clever, so why couldn't I do a sum that Hilary, whom I despised, found the easiest thing in the world? The sense and fear of failure grew in me like a canker. I had never learned how to *apply myself* to things I found difficult. My brain was so full of ideas, fancies and diversions that I was unable to clear away the clutter from my untidy brain and concentrate.

Later, when attempting to teach an able and heavily pregnant fifteen-year-old how to work out percentages and add and subtract fractions, I found myself floundering again. I went to my old friend, Jan, whose approach was astonishing in its simplicity and effectiveness. She greeted any difficulties of mine with cries of glee. I was presenting her with a real challenge. Great! Together we would solve it. Every time I got stuck it was if I had given her a gift. No exasperated sigh, no impatient sneer, nothing negative got in the way of my learning. Suddenly, it all became clear. It was possible for me to do it after all. This attitude rubbed off on her three children, who all did exceptionally well at school and maintained a strong belief in themselves.

Miss Cathcart, with her henchwoman, Hilary, made my schooldays a misery. But worse was to come. Miss Maude, no mean mathematician herself, took over the top classes to allow Miss Cathcart to concentrate on the lower ranks. Miss Maude struck terror into her pupils through her sheer presence. A little over five feet in height, with a face like Tenniel's drawing of the Duchess in Alice in Wonderland, but with a mind as sharp as a razor, Miss Maude made up in bottle for anything she lacked in appearance. Charisma in a head is fine, up to a point, but it was to her disadvantage that she remained with her sisters very cut off from the outside world, especially in relation to the sexuality of her pupils and their needs. She promoted a Victorian ethic in an era when rock and roll was making headway, and it was an unhappy clash of values. Some of the parents of the boarders who had placed their daughters there in the hope that their honour and virginity would be protected while they went about their diplomatic missions elsewhere in the world, were reminded from time to time that girls can climb out of windows, summon youths from the village by phone to fetch them and spend the night at a pyjama party. Miss Maude had never heard of pyjama parties. She was soon given information about them, by someone who spied for the headmistress in the town. We never discovered who it was. The miscreants were summoned and chastised, the daygirls who helped them escape were sent home for a few days. They could not send back the boarders to Hong Kong, Lagos and Malta quite so easily, but Miss Maude made sure their lives were made as unpleasant as possible.

Miss Maude used the old-fashioned words *cheap, common, not nice* and *unladylike*, to describe the practices these girls got up to. Little did she know that it was also going on under her very nose, with her favourite member of staff.

As an all female establishment, the element of backbiting and bitchiness sometimes made us long for masculine company. We found it on the school trip to Venice, in the year that a hit single, Sedaka's 'One Way Ticket to the Blues' topped the charts. Hearing it, I see the sunlit Lido at Easter, with young Italian men who all had names like Rinso, Gino and Carlo flirting outrageously with us, and who declared themselves in love with Lesley, Pamela and June. What could be more romantic than Venice, the Lido di Jesolo and soulful eyed, silver-tongued Italian boys looking for a good time with these English schoolgirls? And the words of the song fade in my mind, like yellowed writing bleached by the sun, but they conjure up the sadness and the melancholy of adolescent love and yearning.

It had begun even before we arrived in Venice. The train had filled up with soldiers on leave who wanted to share our compartments. This was exciting enough and as Maude chased them away, we preened in the mirror and made trips to the toilet, hoping to go past them. It continued from the moment we arrived at the station and saw the magic of the canals, the gondolas and the water taxis, and despite staying in a guesthouse run by nuns, we were watched every second we were there. We were to be housed on the third floor and there were no other buildings close by. We were all weary and tired after spending a night on the train to get there, entertaining soldiers, and we began undressing quite unselfconsciously. Janet and I had been bought our first really pretty clothing by our mother for the trip; we each had a light rayon flower patterned garment to wear over our night attire. The garment did not quite aspire to being a negligee, nor was it thick enough to be a housecoat or dressing gown. Mine was pink, with little pockets, and floated around me prettily as I walked. For the first time in my life, I owned a garment that other girls coveted.

Someone screamed that two men were watching us from a distant balcony with binoculars trained on our windows. Rude gestures appeared to do nothing to change the situation, so we had to close the shutters each time we were in the room. In St Mark's Square it was the same. A target for all the young men with our purple blazers or cardigans and Miss Maude clucking round like a mother hen unable to tell them to go away. The youths pinched bottoms, leered, winked and rubbed themselves up and down our bodies the moment we turned our backs. At first exciting, it began to get quite tedious. For Maude it must have been a nightmare. No matter where we went, they would follow. I fancied myself in love with the handsome young bead seller in St Mark's Square and spent all my pocket money on ropes of pink and blue glass beads, which I still have, just to admire him at close quarters. It was all innocent, of course. We would never have crossed over that line that divided pseudo-mature fourteen- and fifteen-year-olds from knowing and sexually experienced eighteen- and nineteen-year-olds. No contraception was available to us; condoms were not available in many Catholic countries, and anyway, sex was not what we were seeking; what we wanted was the sexual thrill of the chase, the romance, the intrigue, the undercover liaison. I observe this behaviour today in young Muslim girls as they giggle and whisper and titter and hide in corners with their friends, and forge romantic attachments with young men they hardly know. We were like this and expected to remain virgins at least until after we had left school, and preferably until marriage. The thought of becoming pregnant with no husband to support you was shame itself. Of course it happened, but we were affected by the snobbery that goes with being a middle-class girl in a fee-paying school and one didn't do that sort of thing.

There were now a number of girls at the school whose parents were 'in trade'. Their parents had money, but it was clear that the school accepted them on sufferance. They had smart clothes and knew nothing about the genteel poverty of families such as mine. The Misses Potts didn't know how such people worked; their values were not the same. They had no wish for their girls to learn Latin, or botany, but hoped they'd learn domestic science and enough English and maths to get by. They were car dealers, pub landlords, builders and mechanics. They wanted to buy their daughters the best their money could pay for, and in this case, the social standing and peer group came before the educational opportunities offered at the school. Their confidence, unlike ours, was not eroded by looking shabby. Their parents had the confidence of the nouveau riche, and I envied them, though I, with the rest of my family, clung on to the pretence of *us being better than them*, so cherished by my mother. Our family was in a difficult situation; it was a family with pretensions to gentility, fallen on hard times. It took me years to untwist the social constraints and double standards enough to eradicate most of the snobbery and humbug from my own life. At the time of the Venice trip, Father was then in his secondhand car business and the garage was losing money. I don't know where they found the money to send us; possibly it was money my mother had saved.

The school trip went from bad to worse. Two girls went missing on the last evening and the exhaustion of minding the rest of us made Miss Maude physically ill. The girls returned unharmed, but it was the last school trip we ever went on. The ferry crossing on the homeward journey was terrible; the boat pitched and rolled and the waves threw spray over the decks as the lurching stomachs of thirty girls and their teachers emptied themselves over the side, only to have the vomit blown back at them across the decks. Going down below was worse; the hot, oily smell of the throbbing engines induced queasiness in all who ventured below, even without the tossing of the ship on the stormy sea. Miss Maude went a colour as close to green as it's possible for a human being to be. Always sallow skinned, her face took on a ghastly pallor that made her pupils feel protective and genuinely concerned about her for once, an experience she may not have enjoyed, with her strong need to be in charge.

She could not worry about our morals for once; in any case we were as sick as she was. We raved about the holiday afterwards—the light on the lagoon, the romance of the gondolas, Murano, Burano, St Mark's—even the turgid Tiepolos and Veroneses in the Doge's Palace were recalled, memorised and tucked away for future reference. Travel is never wasted on the young.

Back at school, we still had to endure the personal insults and sudden mood changes of the more unbalanced staff. Miss Whitley-Smith, a stout, steel-grey-haired woman of uncertain age, dressed always in tweed skirts and grey cardigans, insulted us on a daily basis.

"Guttersnipes!" she screamed at us, in her thick Derry accent, moustache quivering with rage. "Don't think I don't know what's going on in your mind. God is watching ye." And she would wag her finger at the offenders and glare round the class, daring one of us to break the silence. She was adamant that her hometown, Londonderry, was the most beautiful of places, putting to shame our English cities. She emphasised the 'London' part of Derry, her Protestant fervour bursting forth as she ranted about the Cat'olics and their evil ways. All the venom of the bigot expressed itself in the thick accent, which sounded as if a poisoned potato was being held against the roof of her mouth. The historical context of the struggle, which none of us understood, was frequently blasted at our unwilling ears. There was a feeble protest from an Irish Catholic girl at one point. We all turned round in amazement. She had hardly ever opened her mouth in our company before, but at that moment, she became our hero. Dissenting murmurs were heard around the classroom. The gimlet gaze and steely mouth did not waver. The rant continued.

"Are ye Cat'olic? Well, I'd expect this type of rudeness from the likes of ye. Guttersnipes, ye are." Only when the girl began to cry, did Miss Whitley-Smith desist, and by that time, several other girls were protesting more loudly. From then on, it was open warfare.

Until then Miss Whitley-Smith had kept order in her classrooms through a combination of extreme fear, rote learning and bribery. It worked quite well in some respects and my spelling, vocabulary and ability (now lost) to parse complex sentences, improved dramatically. We had to learn poetry by heart and she was knowledgeable about the work we read, mostly her favourites from Rhyme and Reason, a book standard in schools at the time. I came across a copy recently and was able to admire the choice of work in this anthology, which offered something on every level. The poem by Yeats *An Irish Airman Forsees his Death* had a special resonance for Miss Whitley-Smith and she became quiet when this was read aloud, moved by some memory of home.

When she was thwarted, or suspected a pupil wasn't working hard enough, she became a bully, and terrorised them. It was the term 'guttersnipe' that finally undid her. Word got back to Miss Maude about it, and she reprimanded Miss Whitley-Smith, who took the opportunity to retire, hurt. Many a girl had broken down in tears faced with an incomprehensible text, or difficult spelling, fixed by the gimlet eye, and stabbed by the wounding tongue of Miss W.S. and no one was very sorry to see her go.

There were several weird biology teachers, poor washed-up souls who had travelled the world and been forced to admit defeat. One, whom I will call Miss F, had what appeared to be an unusual tropical skin disease, which so disfigured her face that one became distracted by it and forgot to listen to what she was saying. This was a pity because she was a real enthusiast for her subject and had some wonderful tales to tell about Africa and about the marching armies of soldier ants, unusual creepy crawlies and the plant-life of the Congo basin. Her attempts to keep order were not a success, and I made the mistake of expressing interest in her subject, so that she paid me an embarrassing amount of attention. This, of course, earned me the taunts of the other girls. I got out of the difficult position of being teacher's pet by opening a jar of cockroaches, at her request, for us to dissect, and showering the room with them. This was not deliberate; the largest cockroach's leg had become caught in the cork lining of the jar lid. When I pulled the lid off, the cockroach was flung across the room, while I somehow managed to tip out some of the remainder in my panic. The screaming of my classmates was quite gratifying, as they thought I had done this on purpose.

The second biology teacher was tall and thin and had huge feet, made even more enormous by her rat-trap sandals and skinny white legs. Her way of surviving in the hell-hole of Wendlesham Hall was to smile constantly and allow nothing to upset her. It was a constant challenge. We stole food off her plate, added our own disgusting piles of cabbage when she wasn't looking, stuck bits of paper on her back, and generally tried to make her life a misery. None of it worked. I never saw her angry or upset. The other teachers were made of sterner stuff. They challenged us academically and personally, especially the English teachers, and made us work hard for them. The geography teacher, Miss R., who also taught what was then known as R.E., was not inspiring, but was confident in her knowledge of her subject and did not get drawn in by any of our nonsense. My enduring memory of her is of her standing with one foot on the rung of a chair, her right hand inside her blouse as she massaged the spot just above her left breast. It was almost Napoleonic, and she would gaze into the distance as she stood in this posture, telling us about the cocoa beans in Ghana, the cotton, copra, sisal and tea from wherever they came from, and occasionally show us a sample or two of these products. I retained some of what she taught us, plus a lie, which was that the cotton towns of Northern England are grey miserable places not worth visiting. I have since realised that she spoke with the typical Southerner's prejudice about these matters, but I had to live there to find out the truth.

When I finally left the school, with a respectable number of 'O' and 'A' levels, I felt as though most of my learning had been useless information. It had very little application to the life I wanted to lead. I couldn't wire a plug, write a C.V, cook anything except scrambled eggs, budget on a weekly wage or add up numbers, particularly if I was being watched. On the other hand, I could identify most wild flowers, catch fish and shellfish and cook them, pluck and draw a pheasant, make jam and sew my own clothes, if inexpertly. I could also find my way around outdoors even on a pitch black night with no moon, find lizards and snakes wherever they were to be found, row a boat and ride a bicycle. I was hopeless at tennis or rounders, but was a fast runner, able to vault and climb. I could write imaginative, grammatically correct prose, yet couldn't manage simple office tasks in my first job as a bank clerk. I had a well-developed sense of self-preservation, and needed it. It was translated in my family as selfishness and self-importance, but, in fact, it was a strong drive to be myself, disentangled, as much as was possible, from the unhealthy relationships (or non relationships) the family offered. I would not side with one against the other; I would instead be myself and forge my own path. It was desperately hard at times, with no friendly adults behind me to encourage or advise me. I envied friends who had parents they could talk to. My mother, poor soul, had no understanding of the world I was living in and could not advise me, though she often condemned what I did, and her criticism was usually based on incomplete understanding. My father was more helpful, seldom condemning and occasionally offering support. But his own needs were so great that he had little emotional space for anyone except himself.

I had few close friends at school when I was eight or nine, but there was one girl I felt strongly in sympathy with, and that was Maeve. Irish, freckled, with a rich accent and sporting a school uniform almost as shabby as my own, Maeve had instant appeal. She had ink stains on her summer dress, climbed trees with the skill and grace of a boy and got into regular fights with anyone who crossed her. It was her tree climbing exploits that got us both into trouble. When Maeve fell awkwardly from a low branch and broke her arm quite badly I, as an onlooker, was in trouble again. Why had I been with her? Surely I knew the tree was out of bounds? I should not have been leading her astray.

I picture her now, satchel askew, hair untamed in ribbons that kept sliding loose, dress stained with fountain pen ink, her open face freckled and pugnacious. After her arm was broken, she was at home for weeks, and I missed her. Realising she had borrowed a ruler of mine, I went to her desk to retrieve it in her absence. It wasn't there, but I was interrogated about my actions by a teacher who saw me. Why had I gone to her desk? Was I stealing something? Maeve had been bullied a lot, it seemed, and I was to be branded one of the bullies. In vain, I protested that she and I were friends; that I had merely tried to retrieve something already mine. Finally I was believed, but the guilt and injustice I felt over this and her broken arm destroyed the friendship after she returned.

Another friend I had, Liz, liked fighting almost as much as Maeve. What they both had in common were strong, emancipated mothers who wouldn't take any nonsense from any man or woman. Some of this must have rubbed off on their daughters, and it certainly attracted me. I wanted to admire my mother, wanted her to stand up to my father and tell him strongly and assertively where he got off, and to claim her right to her own life. I wanted her to have more self-respect, and for him to stop bullying her. The anger I felt with my family expressed itself through fights and long, lonely walks. I fought Liz often; she must have had a similar need, and I had not learned self-control. We rolled over and over on the grass, hair being tugged out and clothing torn in the process. She never appeared to bear me any ill-will afterwards. Not so with the village girls.

My sister and I were almost the only children in the village who went to an independent school. Our uniforms—purple blazer, straw boater, navy serge gymslip or mauve summer dress, made us a very visible target and proclaimed to the world at large that we considered ourselves a cut above the ordinary folk in the village.

Two of the village families were larger than average, with children ranging from the eldest who was inevitably in Borstal or doing National Service, to a babe in arms, dressed in the ill fitting clothing of the older siblings. Gilly was my age, and physically we were well matched. She accosted us, with a crowd of smaller jeering children, as we strolled in our uniforms from the bus stop towards our house.

"Come on! Scared to fight, girl? Posh bitch." My hat went flying. I tugged at Janet.

"Let's get home."

"Scared! Running off home to Mummy!" One of them was in my satchel, prising it open.

"Get off!"

"Scared to fight! Posh snobs," holding her finger under her nose in mockery. "Cowardly custard." There were more tugs at my satchel.

I hit her. It was a straight punch to her chest. Her ten-year-old body fell backwards; her face registered surprise. We fought, until we were finally dragged out of the path of an oncoming bus by a passerby. My fights with Janet and at Wendlesham Hall had toughened me. I was no wimp. I could take pain and getting dirty. I had learned that in order to gain respect, a fight was sometimes necessary first.

The fighting is more civilised these days, but it's remained a part of my life. The role of subservient little woman would never be for me, and I am thankful for it.

It was after this physical grappling with 'the village children', as my mother called them that I tried to share some of what we had with them. I invited several children I had begun to get to know, up to the house. They trailed behind me, uneasily, admiring the grey parrot and the enormous garden. My mother told me never to bring them again. They lived in council houses, she said, looking shifty, and might be dirty, thieving or untrustworthy. I logged this information, which to me even at that age made no real sense, for future reference. I was crestfallen and uncomprehending; mother was uneasy and nervous. Mrs. Gadsworth, our daily help, was a woman my mother really respected, in fact long after she had left our employment, my mother visited her and enjoyed her company, but she didn't live in a council house. Mrs. Gadsworth wasn't an educated woman and her malapropisms were delicious at times—escaped budgies hoovering in the trees was one example, but she had dignity and pride. Was this what distinguished her from the village families? I couldn't work it out. But Mrs. Gadsworth was fierce in her condemnation of the two particular families we had fought with and that was enough for my mother. Local families were like tribes. Upset one and you upset them all. Lads from these families who had done National Service were treated with respect, but they generally moved away as soon as they could, continuing with an army career. The ones who went to approved schools left to go to adult jails, though a few managed to survive the lack of opportunity and lack of excitement in the Village. People were willing, on the whole, if they knew someone, to give them the benefit of the doubt if they looked as though they might become honest hardworking citizens, and integration was possible even for those with a long previous history.

The unfortunate Branwell family, an inbred and not terribly bright family who lived in a squalid council house, usually had one member at large in the community who needed the active support and help of the neighbours. Timmy Branwell was known to everyone in the village, a large chap with a malformed head whose problems with his teeth and palate made it difficult for him to be understood. Timmy was known as 'the dotty boy,' not as a taunt, but as a way of distinguishing him from his brother, who was slightly less intellectually handicapped and more prone to violent gestures. The brother was often locked up, partly for his own protection, as he had committed some offences against children, mainly exposing himself. We didn't make much of this, we just avoided him, and in a village this wasn't hard to do. There was a general realisation that some people will not be changed by punishment, but in a small community they can be protected from themselves and others by watchfulness, and one learned to live with them. I don't remember Timmy being teased by local children, I don't think the adults would have allowed it. In those days, there were women at home who looked after the likes of Timmy Branwell, his brother and his sister Mildred, and in this respect, the village was a little like a large family, with the very old being cared for by their neighbours and women 'popping across' at lunchtime to see that old Walter or Elsie was properly fed. With little social care available, these communities looked after their own, as they do today in some communities, but when the first commuters arrived and set up home, it spelled the end of this social cohesion, as the commuters went to work in London and their wives formed a small group of outsiders who did not involve themselves in community affairs, sending their children to the local independent schools and not offering their services to the cricket club or the WI.

These women were lonely, as people are where they move into an area where everyone knows one another and is not anxious to include them.

The social divisions were such that mixing between council house tenants and their children, and the home owning middle and upper classes, was unheard of in our village. The farm labourers and agricultural workers who lived in the tied cottages were a class above the council tenants, but we were not encouraged to mix with them either. In fact, there were precious few children we could mix with, with our parents' approval. My father was more able to tolerate and even embrace difference than my mother, but he rarely argued with her about this.

Once, when he had built up a business relationship with several car dealers in a local town, he discovered that they had daughters attending Wendlesham Hall. With typical social clumsiness he arranged for us to meet them, without consulting us, or my mother, who thought their fathers common and would have nothing to do with them. The meeting was not a success, though the girls were friendly, well groomed and well mannered. We were then as snobbish as our mother, and took on her attitudes and values, and this provided a way of keeping people out of the family, and prevented us finding allies in leaving it. My poor mother, blinkered by so many prejudices and false notions about worth and social standing, missed out on so many social occasions as a result of this snobbery. Her attitudes betrayed her at every turn, from describing my prospective father-in-law, a hardworking GPO engineer, as 'a nice enough little man,' to reminding me that the family I was marrying into was definitely 'not county'. Life had moved on, but left her behind. Her deafness meant that many of her assumptions and statements went uncontested—it was too much like hard work for anyone to challenge her.

Yet, when engaged with others in a one to one encounter, where she forgot her social standing, she was capable of instilling great affection. The chains that bound her in her marriage and her life were complex ones, held in place by other family members who did not want their world to change. Enmeshed in this web of fear of the outside and what freedom might mean, my siblings remained stuck until she died. I chose a different route.

My grandmother Bill had also chosen a different route. From a beautiful, spoiled only daughter, well known as a society belle, she married my grandfather at eighteen and gave birth to my father reluctantly a year later. Several affairs followed which led to the breakup of the marriage, then her second marriage to a man with the name of a Victorian villain, Basil Hamborough. Basil had disappeared from the scene by the time we children were born, and my grandmother was living in the South of France, surrounded by admirers and enemies in equal quantities, and attending Jimmy's Bar in Cagnes. Her home was in Tourette-Sur-Loup, in Provence, but she also had a cabin in the Alps Maritimes, at Saint Martin Vesube, where she liked to spend the summer. The first time I remember meeting her, I must have been around eight years old. I must have met her before this, but she was uninterested in us and any meeting we may have had has not stayed in my mind. At Saint Martin, the summer cabin, with its hayloft and cold-water tank outside the back door, was straight out of my Heidi book, and I adored it. The Alpine meadows were alight with tiny jewel like flowers—haresfoot, harebell, gentian, century, purple plantain—so that I felt quite dazzled. We watched the logs being transported on wires down the mountain, admired the icy river with its pink and purple granite boulders, slippery and treacherous, the carpets of wild flowers.

There was a privy with an earth closet, but no bathroom. Bill explained that she bathed in the square rainwater tank, stripping off and getting in without worrying about the shepherd seeing her, a hardened old peasant who treated the sight of this fifty something woman bathing naked in her backyard with typical French indifference. Bill spoke fluent French, and what she didn't know she bluffed her way through. If she had one academic talent, it was that of a linguist, for she moved to Italy later in her life and learned Italian. She was by then well in her seventies.

The hut was primitive but perfect for us children. Even my brother, only just able to walk, tottered up and down the meadows falling at regular intervals but never hurting himself. My father carried him up the mountain at the back of the hut in a rucksack, with us running ahead, Bill with her stick leading the way and my mother trailing in the rear. Bill was robust for her age and adventurous, but gave us short shrift. Whining or complaining was not permitted, a fact which made my mother very uneasy, as she felt she needed to protect our brother from Bill's criticism. My brother, unaccustomed to attention from my father, put up with the rucksack fairly well, though my father had huge blisters on his feet when we came down again. At the top of the mountain were two small icy tarns, and we bathed our feet in the water, to remember forever the relief of cold water on aching toes. The juniper bushes and blueberries were new to me, and I busied myself on the way down by picking blueberries and giving them to Janet and my mother. Bill told me what plants we were passing and later took me out on my own to find wild mushrooms and strawberries in the woods around the hut. She hung the mushrooms on strings to dry in the shed at the back of the hut, ignoring the maggots that infested them. Her view was that the maggots would complete their life cycle and be well gone from the dried up mushroom by the time she came to eat it. Mostly we found ceps, sticky brown mushrooms with spongy pores, which she showed me how to scrape off, and chanterelles. My mother, always alarmed easily, was not happy with these new pursuits of mine, but resigned herself to keeping my brother out of harm's way.

Bill still had the strawberry blonde bobbed hair of her youth when I knew her, and the mobile, slightly cruel mouth set in the perfect features of the beautiful woman she had once been. She was large breasted but wore expensive silk shirts and tailored skirts and trousers which gave her the appearance of being well turned out even on a windy mountaintop. My mother could not have been more different, with her wiry jet-black hair, slimmer build and unhappy combination of cheap clothes. Bill was socially confident to the point of being arrogant; my mother was timid. Each despised the other.

I remember the stay at the hut being a happy time, despite the differences, and it was when we all went back to Tourettes that things began to get unpleasant. We spent a day at the beach, Bill as usual with a complete lack of modesty stripping off and donning a black swimsuit and large red sunhat before swimming far out to sea and sitting there in the water. We were only just able to swim and dipped in and out near the edge. Bill appeared from the sea, dripping and refreshed and demanded to know why my mother was not going in. And what was wrong with Douglas? He should go in too. My mother protested. Douglas was hauled out of his hiding place and stripped off to be taken to the edge of the water. He didn't like this and picking up on my mother's anxiety, began to howl. Bill said firmly that all French children were thrown in to teach them to swim. My mother grabbed Douglas and carried him into the water, wetting her skirts, but she would not let go of him. My grandmother plainly thought she was being over-fussy and protective and despised her even more. My father didn't know whose side to be on.

I see now that my mother's response was a natural one in wanting to protect her little boy, yet there never did come a time when he was encouraged, even pushed, to take normal risks. Even we could not be entrusted to look after him. Her fearfulness may have developed in response to what she perceived as these early threats, but I sense it was tied to her own anxiety about being alone. She had lost her influence over us to some extent; she was not going to allow her baby to escape, and he never did.

Bill was a complex character in many ways, very selfish, yet very sociable, cold towards my father, yet very affectionate towards her cat, which she had left in the care of a neighbour while we had been at the hut. This cat, when we saw it, was rather like its owner. It was big, it had strange yellow eyes that looked different from any cats we knew, and it had ear tufts. It was a golden ginger colour and it spat whenever we came near. Bill explained that it had come from a litter born near the hut, and that the mother, a female farm cat, had been impregnated by a wild cat. Kiki was half wildcat. The vet had jumped back with surprise when asked to treat it and commented that it was one of the strangest cats he'd seen. Kiki refused to let anyone touch him except Bill and had a huge repertoire of hisses, snarls and spits. He vacated the apartment as soon as Bill arrived back with us, and spent his time moodily catching scorpions in the communal garden at the back of the apartment. We thought him marvellous, he was pure spite and anger, bristling with aggression, and no one would get the better of him.

We stayed in a rented ground floor apartment in the block; while Bill lived in her own smaller one upstairs, underneath a woman she referred to as The Crocodile.

Bill's flat was interesting, as all her apartments were, filled with paintings and bold displays of dried flowers and bright rugs. Even her bath was unusual, a rectangular tub lined with blue tiles, in which she would soak for hours at a time. She had many friends and acquaintances who were painters, potters and sculptors, and their work decorated her apartment. She had a good eye and good taste, in that the items she collected have remained visually pleasing and attractive originals. She had met a number of famous or influential people in the South of France in the Twenties and Thirties at various social gatherings, and although she was not a name dropper, nor was she over impressed with fame, I know she met Picasso, Scott Fitzgerald and Hemingway and she and Basil, her second husband, circulated in the smart set on the Riviera until her money ran out and Basil left her for some other woman. I have a painting of Tourettes she gave me when I married, painted by a Texan boyfriend of hers. It's very modern, bold in execution and it still excites me when I look at it. She had what my family liked to call taste, in objects if not in men.

FIFTEEN

We were boarders on several occasions at our school, after that first time, as our mother had operations on her ears that always promised success but delivered nothing except extreme sickness and vertigo when they failed.

I am in bed, in the big dormitory. I have just got comfortable, despite the pronounced dip in the mattress where the springs have gone. I have a brushed nylon nightdress so full of static that sparks come off it when I take it off. The other girls my age are still awake, but in bed. The younger ones in the next dormitory are mostly asleep. There is whispering from the sisters at the end of the room. Out of bed, they go and look out of the window. Miss Maude and her sisters are out. Matron, having performed her duties, will be in her cabin with her daughter, trying to make up to her for the time not spent with her during the day. Phillipa, who is ten, goes to a local school, as it was thought best if she wasn't in her mother's place of work. She resents her mother giving all her time to these other girls. The girls at the window are excited.

"What are you doing?" The girl in the next bed is anxious.

"Going home."

"What? What do you mean?"

"Can't stand it anymore. We're going before the Potts get back." They packed their little cases quickly and tiptoed to the door.

"Where will you go? It's getting dark." Several voices joined in the chorus.

"We'll stay with the Joneses." The Jones family were Romanies who worked and lived on a nearby farm and had a wagon on a patch of land near Wendlesham Hall. The young Jones boy had foxy blue eyes and black hair. I didn't trust him, or maybe I didn't trust myself with him.

"What if they find you?"

"Don't care. Anyway, we're going." They disappeared down the stairs and we watched them go from the window, as they slipped away in the dusk. Several girls were crying, remembering their own longing for their families and frightened for these two sisters, so determined to get away. It was a long time before we got to sleep.

In the morning Miss Maude came up to speak to all of us. She had heard that the sisters had left the school—she did not use the words 'run away'—and she wanted us to tell her exactly what we knew. It seemed as though many girls had heard different stories about the plans of the two sisters. Some volunteered that the Jones family were harbouring them; some said that they had run away to join their parents, others that they had left to visit a relative in Portsmouth. Miss Maude uttered a dire warning.

"If any girl, *any girl*, thinks that it's clever or amusing to leave here without permission, they will be in very serious trouble. Do you understand?" We did. I remembered my own attempts to run away, and the futility of it all. Whatever you felt or thought or said, grown ups always had the upper hand. The two sisters were brought back, temporarily, until their parents could collect them, and they cried like babies. But at least they went home. Knowing we would not be there long, we could stand it, just about, but it was hard, and there was little effort on anybody's part to understand the misery some of the girls endured at being separated from their families. Later, meeting the two girls who had run away, at a school reunion, it was clear that being so abandoned by their mother so young had affected them throughout their lives.

"My children complain," said Mavis, "that I can't leave them alone. I have to know where they are and what they're doing, all the time. And they're grown up. I look after my mother now, but she'll never understand what she did to us. There's no bond there, really."

Hearing the stories of others who had been at the school and who were now looking back, forty or more years later, was comforting in a strange way. I hadn't been as alone as I thought. Others had suffered too, some much more intensely. Some had been expelled, usually for seeking the love and comfort denied them by their families, in the shape of local boys. Some were expelled for resisting the sexual advances of staff members, or for objecting too loudly to unreasonable treatment. One of these unquenchable intelligent individuals is now a barrister; others bided their time and began their proper education once they were able to leave, becoming lecturers, media people, teachers and nurses.

Was it a good education? In some ways it was good, in other ways not. Where it failed completely was in not keeping abreast of the times we were living in, and in recognising the needs of children separated from their families, whose voices were simply never heard. Over and over again the phrase "You had to get on with it," is heard, as a mantra, from girls of this generation. And they did get on with it, as children evacuated in the war had had to 'get on with it.' Later, with a growing awareness of attachment needs and the work of Bowlby, Winnicot and others becoming more recognised, there was more recognition of the long-term damage of separating young children from their carers. Yet we still do it, as many a private boarding school will testify. At seven, my father, grandfather, and mother had been sent away from their homes. Janet and I were to experience the same, albeit more briefly, but my children were never put through this ordeal, so the pattern has now changed for good.

Wendlesham Hall prided itself on the physical education of its girls. The school held a large number of silver cups and shields, awarded annually to girls who excelled at high jump, long jump, hurdles, relay races and sprints. My mother had won the Victor Ludorum trophy for all round achievements whilst she was a pupil, and we valiantly tried to follow in her footsteps. My sister, having longer legs than I, was a good high jumper, while I could vault and run quite adequately. Being shortsighted, I found any racquet games very difficult and hated tennis, netball and hockey, which I considered to be a vicious, barbaric game, involving the bigger girls exposing their mottled purple thighs while they charged around the pitch in the freezing December weather, whacking the ball with a lethal weapon, otherwise known as a hockey stick. I was constantly drawn away by mushrooms growing on the pitch, which I picked to take home, or the seagulls following the plough in the next field — anything to distract me from the tedious humiliation of the hockey match. Things became worse after the arrival of Miss Jones.

Miss Jones was young, in her late twenties, and was small, tough and heavily made up. She was energetic, alarmingly fit and terrifyingly unsympathetic. She chivvied us, forced us to take part in long distance runs, in which we trailed across the cold Hampshire countryside in navy blue knickers and aertex shirts, and shouted at us if we slacked. There was at the time a number of troops from Aldershot on manoeuvres in the area, and the taunts, catcalls and whistles we endured as they drove by in their open backed army lorries, past us plodding, lumpen teenagers in our knickers, had to be endured unless one could find a place to hide. Miss Jones was always at the head of the field and did not appear to mind the catcalls. Miss Jones fluttered her eyelashes at the Misses Potts, stuck out her pointed breasts, and entertained us with tales of minor male celebrities she had been out with. She led us to think she was a sexually active, emancipated, young-thinking woman, a person whom we could admire and aspire to be like.

One sunny day, when we had a long lunch break, it was reported that one of the younger girls, Fern, who excelled at sport, was sunbathing up near the woods with Miss Jones. And they were naked. We didn't believe it, but the girl didn't deny it. We had been aware of letters passing between them, and assignations being made. It became clear to all of us that the relationship between Miss Jones and Fern was more than platonic. The attitude of the other pupils was generally understanding and accepting. Fern was well liked, and it was understood without being greatly discussed that she had been given the body and outlook of a boy, without the testosterone. I don't recall any name calling about this, just an acceptance that this was the way she was. Fern was not complaining about the relationship, though she often seemed unhappy. Who were we to object? This was love, was it not? Then we began to have our doubts. Whatever crisis of gender and orientation she was going through, Miss Jones made sure she felt it keenly. Then Miss Jones chose another victim for her charm offensive and expertly began to play one girl off against another, while keeping her original conquest as the main focus of her attention.

The boarders who were most vulnerable were the ones who were at the school because of some family crisis, and they needed the attention and affection of someone—anyone—like flowers need rain. Miss Jones was expert at manipulating people.

"Come and sit by 'ere, girls," she would call, in her strong Welsh accent, beckoning them to the seat next to hers on the coach to the swimming baths. Meekly they obeyed. She would place an arm round their shoulder in a semblance of protective affection. Trust being won and secrets established, the relationships developed in this way became passionate, full of jealousy and possessiveness, and highly charged with sexual excitement. I was not a part of this charmed circle, being suspicious by nature, and unattractive to look at, but I could see the damage it did to the girls involved. They became consumed by intense sexual feeling and desperate in their need to be needed and loved by someone, even if that someone was the Games Mistress. There were relationships, mostly unconsummated, between girls too, of course, but without the age or power differential. Later I came to see that the techniques employed by Miss Jones were very typical of abusing adults and that it was the vulnerable unconfident pupils who were targeted most often and who may, even now, deny the harm it did them. I'm sure that Miss Jones wasn't the first or only member of staff to initiate a sexual rapport with a pupil, but she was the one whose appetite was most blatantly displayed, basking as she did in the admiration of the Misses Potts. We were all, I think, confused about our own sexual identity then, in this all female hot house, with the absence of protective adult guidance and affection.

I missed affection keenly after I reached puberty; my mother was too annoyed with me to give affection freely and my father did not know how. My developing, badly managed body probably scared them to death. No wonder fantasy flourished and pop stars and film idols peopled our thoughts and dreams.

Another girl was the object of my sexual fantasies for a while, in the absence of male affection, and it didn't help that she was prone to displaying her larger than average breasts quite openly while we changed for PE. I felt disturbed by my own impulses then, but did not act on them and hurriedly looked around for a more acceptable object of desire. It took me a long while to recognise that same sex attraction was going on all around me at the time and was just a normal part of adolescence. However, the joining in of a supposedly responsible adult was a different matter. Her seduction techniques were well honed, on men as well as women, which gave us a false sense of security at the start, but after a while, the situation became too disturbing for it to be ignored any longer. By the time this happened I was, with two friends, at the top of the school and more sure of my ground. Together we discussed how to bring the situation to the attention of the Misses Potts. Finally we involved the father of one girl, a highly respectable professional man whose word would be respected by Miss Maude. Overnight the deed was done, and Miss Jones left the school the next day, amid tears and recriminations, leaving behind a stack of semi pornographic love letters and several brokenhearted and confused little girls. We were ignorant about paedophilia in those days, but trusted our basic instincts, which luckily were sound enough to see us through what I remember as a very difficult time for the three of us.

Single sex schools are always going to attract homosexual staff, and there were a number of talented and dedicated women teachers at Wendlesham Hall who were undoubtedly lesbian. They must have been made quite anxious by the dismissal of Miss Jones.

Miss Maude, faced with the perfidy of her favourite young teacher, (and I ask myself what homo-erotic fantasies were built up between this aging spinster and this dynamic, sexually charged young games teacher), was appalled to discover this aspect of human nature, which, like Queen Victoria, she could hardly believe possible. Surely such things could not have been going on in Wendlesham Hall!

We had heard rumours about male gardeners being encouraged to leave when they were thought to be too appreciative of the charms of the young women in the school. As far as I was concerned, George, the head gardener, and his helpers were part of the landscape, no more an object of lustful desire than my satchel. I liked George; he was a comfortable older man with a grey moustache who smoked a pipe and lent on his spade to watch the robin at his feet investigate the soil for grubs. He was a countryman, taciturn, self-effacing and knowledgeable. The younger gardeners and groundsmen were hard put to it to avoid the giggles and innuendoes of the girls, especially the boarders, who must have made their lives a misery at times. George seemed almost impervious, though he could snap back when really pushed with a "You ought to be ashamed of yourselves," which did have the effect of stopping us in our tracks.

We were led to believe then that men were not to be trusted. We were not to be trusted with them either and now women were also not to be trusted. Who could one have a relationship with? Most of us were lonely, starved of affection, needing a sexual outlet, full of romantic dreams and fantasies, which were totally unrealistic. Not surprising, then, that the epithet *boy mad* was dished out frequently, along with the words *cheap, tarty* and *common*. Distinctions were made between *nice* girls and the rest. It was very clear where Miss Maude's preferences lay.

After the Miss Jones affair, we were forbidden to consort with girls younger or older than ourselves, with all sorts of dire hints and warnings that never quite spelled out what the problem was. I had discovered boys by this time and didn't care overmuch what was going on. I was anyway about to leave in a year's time and I reckoned I could hang on until then.

Because the asthma I had suffered from as a young child had left me a year behind, it was decided that I was possibly bright enough to do A levels, but I would have to do them in one year rather then two. There wasn't much choice of subject. Art, which I loved, was not on the agenda, neither was Biology. There remained a choice between history, French or English. I opted for the latter two, though my French was very weak. There was only one college apart from Wendlesham Hall, in the neighbourhood which offered A levels and it was a long way from our house. There was no encouragement from home to stay on at school, get a job, or try to gain further qualifications. My father's view seemed to be that being female, I would only waste any education by getting married and a safe little job would be the best thing for me for the time being. My mother, who by this time was very depressed and negative about everything, offered no encouragement to do anything.

I stayed at Wendlesham Hall and took French with an elderly Polish émigrée who had come down in the world. She wore beautiful jewellery and claimed aristocratic connections. She was very wise and well read, and she somehow pulled us through Moliere, Hugo, Verlaine, Daudet, Rimbaud and Racine, by making us read aloud in French before translating. Racine I found very dry and over full of classical references, though I might enjoy it now. Verlaine, Baudelaire and Rimbaud I loved, being at an age to appreciate the overblown romantic sentimentality of the poets. If only I could write like that, I thought, surveying *'Les sanglots longs des violins d'automne, Blessent mon coeur d'une langeur monotone ...'* It was exactly how I felt a lot of the time, a sort of languorous melancholy.

In English we studied Chaucer, Blake, Keats and Wordsworth. I learned to admire Wordsworth's grand eloquence in the Prelude, while continuing to despise his melodramatic ditties. But it was Blake who captivated me, as he does most of the young who study him. The Songs of Innocence and Experience spoke to me of my life and my struggles to retain a balance between two situations, whilst losing sight of neither. I was learning a difficult lesson: to accept that the world is not black or white, people are neither wholly good nor wholly bad; everything has two sides. I knew this already, from the struggle between my parents. Loving one and hating the other was never an option for me, though it took leaving home to tell me this for sure. I also understood, with William Blake, Innocence and Experience; the young man on the canal tow-path had destroyed my innocence and sense of security forever and introduced fear into my life. Through the reading I was required to do, I found words of comfort and sustenance which have remained my own personal emotional larder, to be raided in times of hunger.

SIXTEEN

Life at home was difficult in this last year at school. At seventeen I was anxious to try out my wings. I had been to France as an au-pair in a *pension de vacances*, a holiday home for children whose families were working, for several months prior to taking the A level in French. I still failed the oral at the end of the year, but the experience had taught me that I was more competent than I had thought at getting around and fending for myself. Again, my mother's fearfulness transmitted itself to me and became the single biggest barrier to my going, but I managed it for all that, with the school arranging it so that I didn't have to run any unacceptable risks. Having this buffer between myself, and my mother, was helpful for her too, I believe. I came back quite fat, brown, and able to understand spoken French, if not able to speak it very fluently.

Because my mother had lived with my Great-Aunt Ethel from the age of eight until her marriage, almost continuously, she had never really left home herself, in fact, she had moved back into it after my aunt's death. She did not understand the mechanisms by which adults learn to be independent and to make their own way in the world, and she certainly didn't want any of that for us, though on another level, it seemed as though she needed us to take the initiative. If she let us go, she might lose us for good. If she didn't, she would stifle any growth there was in us to make something of our lives. It must have been a terribly painful dilemma for her. My father, the engineer, hardly helped. He had long ago given up the hope that she would take a real interest in his work or social life, and was often out sorting out a music evening, or helping a friend restore an organ, or playing at the local folk club. One of the reasons she didn't ever want to accompany him was that she found him embarrassing. One Christmas he went to the Folk Club party and performed, dressed as a fairy, complete with tutu, wings and wand, a ditty he had composed specially for the occasion, full of smutty humour and innuendo. Similar party pieces included a homemade fart machine, and a complicated box with levers that made quacking, mooing and yowling noises. There were humorous monologues to go with each one. Frank Crumit and Stanley Holloway were favourites of his and he had always played 'The Gay Caballero,' 'The King of Zulu,' and 'Riding Down From Bangor' to us whenever he found he had a captive audience. The other performers in the Folk Club tired of him before long, as he was rarely able to appreciate anyone else's music. Also there was something undignified about a senior citizen, with his big nose poking out from under his sombrero, singing 'The Gay Caballero,' and laughing at his own jokes, because he never knew when to stop. But they were good humoured enough to give him his space and buy him a pint.

When I was eighteen and had left school, I searched around vainly for work that I felt I could do. In the next village was a hard-pressed mother of four young children, whose husband was in the Air Force. They were looking for a mother's help.

The children, ranging in age from six to two, were mischievous, healthy, brown-eyed, little rascals who gave me a run for my money. I babysat for their parents, took them on walks and tried to give their mother a bit of piece over the summer holiday. This all came to an end quite quickly when their father took me home and made a very decided pass at me. I felt outraged and angry, as I liked his wife, who had been good to me and was in the process of showing me, though she didn't know it, an alternative model of mothering. At around this time, Charles came in to my life. In future I would have a reason to fend off the advances of men I didn't like—a boyfriend.

Charles was very good-looking and seemed older than he was, having a wonderful black beard and piercing blue eyes. He was all of twenty. He rode a Norton motorbike and hoped to get a job with the Forestry Commission, having already enlisted as a fire spotter. His parents were academics and even older than mine. His mother, a kind woman, grew wonderful Madonna lilies under the trees in their shady garden. I admired these greatly. It would be good, I thought, to have had a mother who had gone out to work and who was an acknowledged expert at something; one moreover who was quiet but heard every word I said.

After many years of starvation of physical affection, probably for him too, suddenly we could supply this to one another. We could not get enough of one another and suddenly I could see an escape hatch opening up in front of my eyes. He was it. It was a brief but passionate relationship that only ended when he went away to college.

With him I had defied my mother, stayed out late, placed a foot inside the larger world of night clubs, jazz venues and all night cafes, discovered my sexuality and begun to understand that I did not have to keep my place as the buffer in between my parents. They would have to learn to manage without me.

I had found another job by then, in a bank. I hated it from the moment I started, disliking the sneers of the secretary who quickly discovered I couldn't touch type or operate a switchboard, and the nine-to-five routine. I found being indoors all day a real burden, and still do. Only the morning and evening contact with the world outside has made it possible for me to work indoors, at all. I left the bank after a year, before they threw me out and it was a miracle I lasted that long. Part of my training as what was then described as a rem. (remittance) clerk, involved going up to High Holborn and taking part in various training exercises run by a variety of sadistic and humourless personnel. Anything faintly resembling my father's bullying "You're hopeless at that, here let me show you," style was guaranteed to make me fail. Shades of Miss Cathcart and all those other adults who had made me seem like a fool through my schooldays disabled me horribly. I was late on the first morning, being too timid to tell the conductor to put me off at the right bus stop. I couldn't add up the columns of sums they gave us quickly enough, couldn't work the big machine that printed out statements without breaking something, couldn't, in fact, function even normally.

Was I stupid? Was there something wrong with me? No, I was above average in IQ but well below average in mastery of simple tasks, like finding my way from A to B without getting lost, or keeping my train ticket safe. Now, when I find myself rummaging through my purse for something I know was there a second before and then dropping the contents on the floor and becoming irritated with myself and panicky, I tell myself to slow down. I will have something else on my mind, more important than any of this, and I can tell myself to be calm, stay rational and get enough sleep. The missing object then soon appears.

We are left legacies by those who surround us when we are young, legacies of hope, despair, triumph or failure. The messages that came my way were very varied.

My mother said I thought I knew it all. My father kept quiet but muttered darkly about damaged goods and men wanting any old bike to practise on. I found these remarks highly offensive, as I was still technically a virgin, despite the intensity of my relationship with Charles. My mother promoted insecurity by never commenting favourably on what I was wearing or how I looked after I reached eighteen; my father ogled but said nothing. My mother gave dire warnings about getting pregnant, being used by men, being cheap, and criticised my choice of contraception without offering any alternative advice or practical help. I longed for a mother who would trust me to be sensible, give me sound advice and encourage me to pursue my dreams; one I could confide in and could feel loved by. Love had ceased to exist between us except as a concept after I had defied her that night with Charles.

I was not, I am sure, an easy teenager. But I was a fairly normal one. After my mother reached fifty she gave up on life, me, and any plans she had had for me, or for herself. Her father had died at fifty, when she was eight, and her life had died too. What was there to carry on for now she had reached fifty? I needed her there to fight with, since my father was so disengaged. But at eighteen and nineteen, the fights were brutal and damaging. My father did not really back her up; he was frightened of taking us on, knowing that it would only alienate her further.

There is no affection between them at this time. He tries at times to put an arm around her, but she pushes him away. He would say he loved her, but he doesn't really know her. It's what she represents that he needs. She is poor, deaf Edith who would have had no one if it had not been for him. The notion that no one might have been preferable is not one he can tolerate. She certainly says she doesn't love him. It was a mistake and she married the wrong man, is what she says when the chips are down. Yet she can't leave him, being too afraid of hurting him too deeply to allow him to experience abandonment once again. He says the same about her; that he can't leave her, she'd have nobody to look after her. The reflected image these two near-orphans see in one another's faces is stronger than love. They hate what they see, but they cannot abandon it. They cannot part, yet cannot be happy together. Except that there are occasions when both are outside the family home—her house—and my brother and sister are elsewhere. These are rare occasions, but they happen. They even hold hands when thinking themselves unobserved. They go out together and have lunch in the pub; they go shopping. The fact of the house being in trust to my brother means that it can never be my father's home. Although unwilling to take on the responsibility this entails, my brother has the whip hand. He can, if anything happens to his mother, turn his father out. My father is emasculated. He does not have a role, though he would like one as my mother's husband. At home the jealous angry eyes of the brother and sister who can't grow up force her to choose between her husband or her children, and her children win every time. They have to; she feels such guilt at having left them before, she cannot hurt them by telling them to go, to get out of her life so she and my father can be together. Besides, she knows he is a bully; he doesn't make any attempt to cope with her deafness and he is insensitive to a degree. Life without her children would be unbearable, though they are becoming more glum and trapped every day, the older they get. But by then I have gone, to my own life and family, and have left them behind.

SEVENTEEN

The problem is partly sex, I reflect, as I discover the excitement of a close, longed for relationship. My mother is unable to talk about it, except to hint darkly that it's brutish, unpleasant and not to be discussed. My brother's conception was a mistake, she hints, and men are not to be trusted. I have a suspicion that she prefers the company of women, as she lived for a while before her marriage with my godmother, a deeply religious, slightly masculine woman who wore trousers (unusual for that time) and who had a series of younger female companions after my mother. My mother had had no serious boyfriends before my father arrived on the scene. Many women of that age were to be denied marriage and children by virtue of the shortage of men, and had to fend for themselves; opting to live with a female companion as the next best thing. My mother, it seems, was anxious that she should not live her life in spinsterhood. Now she is homophobic.

Closets are firmly shut in those days, and my mother would rather be seen dead than wear trousers, and hisses in loud whispers that a woman in the hospital bed next to hers who is wearing pyjamas is probably a lesbian (we have to shut her up at this point) and voices her disapproval of women whose sexuality seems ambiguous.

I find this interesting, as Aunt Ethel's friend, Gee, lives down the bottom of the garden of the house next door and grows her own tobacco along with her vegetables and smokes it in a pipe. Gee has been given a woman's body, wrongly, in her opinion, as she is almost indistinguishable from a man, in her corduroy breeches and weather beaten face, but she is making the best of a bad job. Gee has a lover, a local librarian many years her junior, who has red hair and who sunbathes on Gee's patio in a small bikini. There is talk about it in the village. I like Gee, she is a change from the other older women in my life and she does not put on an act or talk very much to me if I go down there; she keeps herself to herself. My mother has known and lived next to Gee all her life and takes her masculine traits for granted, but something about lesbians continues to get under her skin. I think my mother knew she had to have sex with a man to get pregnant, but what that entailed she had little idea about and she did not know what to expect on her wedding night, she tells me. But the idea that this might be something to enjoy, the idea of desire, passes her by. After the age of forty, I don't remember her ever showing my father any spontaneous affection. Was she afraid it would lead to sex? Probably. He, on the other hand, showed her affection in the form of sentimental presents or gestures to impress visitors. She always repudiated them. He wanted the world to understand that he was a lover, but his smirk always gave him away. What happened in private no one would know, but they had separate bedrooms after she became ill, and she was relieved not to share his bed.

The house is quiet. I have come home after staying out late with Charles again and my mother is furious.

"Caroline!" I creep downstairs the next morning. It's Saturday and I don't have to go to work.

"What?"

"Don't say *what* to me like that. Where were you last night?"

"Out." I turn away from her, knowing it's an unacceptable answer.

"With Charles I suppose? You'll be getting a reputation." She sniffs, to show she despises me.

"So what?"

"Well if that's what you want ..." She can't think of another comment to make. I go after her.

"Just because you never go out."

"What's that supposed to mean?"

"Well, you don't, do you? I'm supposed to hang around here like you do. Well, I won't. Dad doesn't." This is true; he is often out at one of his clubs, or sorting out someone's heating system, organ or hi-fi. Anything rather than be at home.

"Your father has no idea. He leaves everything to me." This is true to some extent. To her dying day she insists she had to 'row the boat all the way' for the family; that he is useless, a liar, untidy, untrustworthy, doesn't listen, is always late, you can't trust a word he says, is gullible, muddled in his thinking and has no friends. Some of this is true, but none of it is *all* true.

"He's not all bad. Anyway, he goes to work, he can't do everything."

"Oh, he works when it suits him."

"What's that supposed to mean?" She sniffs again, loudly, always her way of showing disapproval. She is always aware of her economic stratus and her lack of any work history. This puts her at a great disadvantage with us, as she has no real idea about the way the world works outside the home. She is very cut off from the mainstream of life, both by her deafness and by being geographically isolated. Although she can and does drive, our house is some way from the town, and her driving is rather erratic. The main problem is that she is unable to hear the noise of the engine and has no idea when to change gear. She cannot hear the protesting clutch or the grating gearbox. My father tries to look after her cars for her, but receives little thanks.

He was still working when I left home, as a central heating engineer, and he made enough money to pay the bills and keep us in food. Later he was offered work in Ireland and the Lebanon, servicing and repairing the new packaging machines now shrink-wrapping produce for the market. He understood how such machines worked, as he did every machine I saw him come across. He was paid well for these excursions, but my mother was not happy.

"What does he want to go to Ireland for?" she said. "He's got enough to do here." Nor would she share his excitement with these trips. When he returned from Lebanon, he brought her a present, a music box inlaid with bone and sandalwood. She sniffed as she opened it and put it on the window-sill, where it remained unopened and untouched, a symbol of their relationship, until she died. He had wanted her to be delighted with the gift, or show some appreciation for his thought, but she was unable to. He turned down further offers of work abroad after this. His gloom deepened.

Gradually as his workload decreased, he began to spend more time at home. At first, his main domain was the shed, which he filled with plumbing parts, ancient boilers and an enormous number of tools, pieces of wood, formica and metal that he thought might come in handy. The robin had a nest in a glue pot on a high shelf, and was left undisturbed. The shed was cold in the winter, and he came in to use the old dining room more and more, which he had taken over as an office some years ago. This was the room referred to as 'Father's pigsty,' and became a no-go area for the rest of the household. When he semi-retired from work, he found the pigsty too cramped and uncomfortable. He couldn't find anything. He moved by degrees into the living room, where he had a television, his home assembled hi-fi, his record collection and a cosy fire. The rest of the family, who did not want to share a room with him, was forced to either confront him or crowd into the small breakfast room, which had another television and one easy chair. My brother stayed in his own room most of the time, my sister was out, my mother was isolated. My father sat in solitary splendour in the living room, hoping others would join him, but they never did. Gradually the table became covered with papers and press cuttings, music magazines and pieces of sheet music. He would be in this room until bedtime, some while after midnight, sucking on his pipe or snoring, his long legs stretched out in front of the fire, hands folded protectively over his stomach. He would always deny he had been asleep, but would wake with a start if disturbed.

To enter this room felt like intruding on personal space; yet the room had previously been used by all the family. Suddenly this ceased to be the case. He did not like the programmes my mother watched and called them rubbish. She disliked the music he played and later the German or Austrian stations he recorded, which had concerts of waltzes and popular music. There was no live and let live, no give and take, on either side. I never knew him to watch or listen to anything she was interested in, yet he expected her to share his enthusiasms.

As a child, the one thing about my father that was most difficult for us was his habit of always being late. It amounted at times to a sadistic need on his part to make us suffer. Speech Day at school happened once a year. There were always events happening that we were involved in, as performers or participants, and to be late was the worst of all possible sins. We would tell him this, sometimes even insisting we had to be there earlier than in fact we did, but it made no difference.

We are dressed in clean, pressed school uniforms. My mother is looking attractive, with a little pink-feathered hat that contrasts well with her black hair, and a dark grey dress, padded and gathered at the shoulders. She has a less visible hearing aid these days, tucked behind her ear. We go out to the car, teasing our brother and making him squeal a little. We wait, fidgeting. Father comes out. We don't believe it; he's almost on time. He looks as though he's about to get in the car, then changes his mind. He's wearing a navy pinstriped suit that doesn't fit well. He goes to the front of the car and lifts the bonnet.

"What's the matter now?" enquires my mother, impatience in her voice.

"Just checking the oil." He pulls the dipstick out and inspects it. He takes a dirty piece of rag from his pocket and wipes the dipstick, then puts it back.

"Please, Dad, can we go? We'll be late." He ignores us. He goes into the shed and after an interminable age reappears with an oil can. Our mother is beside herself.

"Can't it wait, Arthur? You'll make your suit filthy." He enjoys watching us squirm. Eventually he can find no other excuse and gets in, with excruciating slowness, and drives us with reluctance to our school. We are all by then hot and bothered, as my mother would say, and my brother is crying to go to the toilet. Sometimes we slip in unnoticed, sometimes we are told off for being late. We want to shout that it's not our fault. It really isn't fair.

He does the same on holiday, once setting off so late for the ferry that when he gets there the boat is about to sail. An argument ensues. Undeterred, he drives halfway onto the boat, with us inside, unsure whether to laugh or cry. My mother, once again, is not amused. He is late for meals almost as a deliberate act, even if he's in the house. Again, this form of torment for my mother is awful to witness. We tell her to put his dinner on the table and let it go cold, but no, she keeps it hot and has to jump up from her own meal to serve him. He comes in long after everyone else has sat down, smirking and insisting he didn't know dinner was ready. I almost find it funny, it's so predictable, but I also know that I will never allow this kind of game playing to rule my life. It takes me years to shake off the effects, however, and I still panic when I have to be somewhere and think I might be late. I establish a pattern of family meals with our own four children that is very different from the anxious, stress laden occasions I recall from my childhood. Having little money, I learn to make a little meat or fish go a long way, and my children all eat the same things. If they don't like it, they go hungry, but they never do. Family meals are pretty relaxed on the whole, whereas for my mother, they must have been a nightmare.

My father's dietary requirements were that he never ate rice, (it looked like maggots), spaghetti, (it looked like worms), mutton, curry, any other pasta, green vegetables, (they gave him wind) or anything that reminded him of his boarding school. My brother refined his choice of food to only eating peas, bacon, fish-fingers, sausages and chips, with an occasional grape or ice cream as a pudding. My sister was vegetarian, but often cooked her own food. My poor mother was faced with the chore of providing several menus on a tight budget and got no thanks for any of it. I know she wished she could clear off and leave us to cook for ourselves, but my brother, who was the most restricted in his eating habits, was never criticised for this, though my father often was.

EIGHTEEN

At eighteen and nineteen, I constantly felt myself to be the go-between.

My father accosts me in the living room. My mother is working in the kitchen. This is the last bit of her territory; she has to share the rest with us, or surrender it to him. He looks at me sorrowfully.

"Ask your mother what she wants for her birthday."

"Why can't you ask her?"

"I never get any sense out of her. She won't tell me."

I go into the kitchen where my mother is getting supper. I stand just in front of her so she has to look up.

"Mum, Dad is asking what you would like for your birthday." She looks sideways, unhappily. Even here she can be got at.

"Tell him not to bother. I'm all right." This won't do. I try again.

"There must be something you need that he could get you?"

"Never mind." This is her way of dismissing both me, and the subject. "If I tell him something, he'll only get it all wrong."

"If you tell me exactly what you want, I'll try and see he gets it." But she won't play ball. I know that if he does not buy her a present, he will be in the wrong, and if he does buy her a present, he will not get it right either. He can't win. Eventually I pin her down, and tell him that what she would like is a pair of black leather gloves, medium size. Surely he can't get that wrong. But he does, he buys her slippers, the wrong size and with fur round the edges, which she hates. He claims he couldn't find any plain black gloves at a reasonable price. I vow never to play the message carrier again. He buys what he thinks she should have, rather than what she wants. It's typical of him.

They don't communicate; he won't take the time to speak to her so that she can hear him, she won't speak to him, in case he reads it as encouragement to tell her all about his various ailments or his bowels, or old Tony's organ, or his childhood holidays in the South of France. She is deaf to him, as he has been deaf to her needs. I find the pair of them exasperating, but find that my mother's extreme negativity is more dangerous because of what it does to my brother and sister, but my father's total disregard for the feelings of other people and inability to try to change anything is equally culpable. She can't help being deaf. He, I reluctantly grow to realise, can't help having this dangerous narcissistic personality. Feeling himself slighted or alone, he tries by desperate means to turn the spotlight back on to himself. He threatens suicide, obliquely and with no real intention of carrying it out. Each time we part he says, "I don't think I've much time left. Something tells me that I won't be around much longer." Twenty years later, he is still saying the same. I point out, gently, that he is actually getting nearer to the time when that will be true, but to make the most of every day he has. Every time I go back, we repeat the performance.

When he has attention and affection he becomes less needy, but he still can't reciprocate. All through his childhood, he was the one there under sufferance, not wanted or loved by his mother or stepmother. Here he is again in his wife's house, under sufferance, not wanted or loved. He knows he belongs here.

Later, when I am in my thirties and my brother is twenty-nine, my brother becomes very depressed, going to his bedroom for long periods of time and eating little. For once, the subject is discussed when I am there with them. We sit round the circular dining table.

"Douglas hasn't been well." My mother whispers this loudly, in response to a query about his whereabouts, gesturing upstairs to where my brother's room is.

"Why, what's the matter?" I ask. My father looks as though he's about to give a pronouncement but doesn't.

"Depressed," hisses my mother, mouthing it at me. My father chips in.

"I'm sorry to hear that." Didn't he realise, then? Clearly not.

"Do you know what about?" I ask. She doesn't. I tell them, since she's expecting some sort of diagnosis from me, that he's a young man who is not doing the things young men do. Perhaps he shouldn't be at home any longer? My mother, who still makes my brother's bed, cooks his meals and does his washing, looks as though I'd stabbed her in the heart.

"Where would he go? This is his home."

"He has no friends, no social life, no fun, no freedom. He can't have that here."

"He has got friends. He gets cards from people at work at Christmas. I wish he could drive. That would make such a difference. Anyway you always think you know the answer."

"Well, you asked me so I told you." My father weighs it up.

"There may be something in what you say," he concedes. "I was in digs when I was younger than Douglas. Wasn't allowed to bring girls home." And off he goes down memory lane, about his grandmother, his girlfriend, his Peterborough friends.

"To get back to Douglas..." But my mother isn't listening. She cannot face the realisation that she needs him right there with her, to over-mother and indulge. How can she let him go? She can't. Besides, he'd never cope out there away from her.

And if he left, she would have only my father for company. I do sympathise, but frustration with this stuck and lethal need that is robbing my brother not only of his health but his adult life, finally makes me write to him. He does not reply.

There is a saying in the North that it's a poor chick that cannot peck for itself. Instead of leaving home, my brother takes up astronomy and long distance running, both of which fill a need to escape temporarily from home life. After a while, they cease to be effective and something in him dies, as his life is taken over by an illness which leaves him tired, aching and weak. Strangely, the symptoms vanish when he goes on holiday.

When I left the bank, I had been going out with Charles for eighteen months. He began a college course for the Forestry Commission in Wales, and the distance took its inevitable toll. I was devastated when it ended. Where was my prop now? He had provided me with a third space, neither at home nor alone and I acknowledged my need for that. I had several other boyfriends, one of whom was desperate to find a wife, as he was thirty. Almost anyone would do, I felt. In vain he took me to visit various married couples he knew in Surbiton and Banstead, in the hope that I might recognise the attractions of being married. I ended it with a letter, and I hope I wasn't too unkind and that he a found a loyal and faithful wife. I had learned that it is harder to end a relationship with a man who has become dependent on you but whom you do not love, than to be cast aside by a lover you adored.

I decided to make a complete break of it, and applied for various residential jobs in children's homes and charities. I remember my despair at being shown round a home for children who were suffering from brain abnormalities. A severely hydrocephalic baby was lying in a cot in a room with another who had a miniscule head. Neither of them seemed capable of smiling or recognising their surroundings. There was nothing for them to look at or do and although they were clean and well cared for, the soulless nature of the place depressed me for days after my visit. I knew I could not work there, yet felt extremely guilty for saying that. I realise now that this was a home where children were put by their parents to die. They were the secret children, hidden from the world. Eventually I was taken on by a charity working with refugees and their parents and remained there until I decided to go to college and become a teacher.

At twenty-one, I was ready to go to college. London awaited me, with all its challenges and excitement. The interview was a farce. We were a motley crew who took part in this, the last interview of the year, when they were filling up their extra places. A butcher's boy, a London cabbie, a Sikh woman defying her parents, a Sloane debutante, an anarchist painter, a fat lay preacher from Wales, an African potter, a Scots miner—the mixture was a very assorted one and I loved it. It was exactly what I needed. Father grumbled about education being wasted on a woman and would not give me his contribution, my mother discouraged me, but here I was, in London in the Sixties, free at last.

Two boyfriends later, I began to realise that what I needed from a man was constancy and the ability to be a good father—better than mine, at any rate, though I recognised he hadn't been abusive, just inept and inadequate.

THE ENGINEER'S DAUGHTER

Together with Jacky, I watched the next year's intake arrive at the college. Positioned in the refectory, we watched these self-conscious new entrants as they ran the gauntlet of our stares down the long gangway to the counter. I was struck by the determined walk and self-possession of one young man. Of average height, with long hair, glasses and sporting a crumpled corduroy jacket, I knew that this man was interesting. Our children comment that he looked like Jarvis Cocker, but his smile was warmer and his personal style contained and yet open. I joined a drama group he belonged to and looked at him from close quarters. I still liked what I saw. Then I discovered that he had been a school-friend of a friend of mine. I made some enquiries and was told that he was trustworthy and had worked in several tough play schemes and youth groups in different parts of England before coming here. I was impressed. His work history was much longer than mine, even though he was a year younger than me. He drove, had lived away from home for years, had worked since he left school at fifteen, and had a sense of his own worth and integrity. He had a blind older brother up at Oxford, with whom he went cycling and to jazz clubs. His concern for others was very appealing. And he was only twenty-one. I offered myself to him at a drunken party and he accepted, and our fates were sealed.

Jacky, always very smart and well dressed, educated me in the ways of London life. Her parents lived in a small privately rented flat in Ealing, and she knew her way around London, having worked at County Hall for several years after leaving school. She took me on trips to Biba and Kensington High Street, showed me pubs by the river at Richmond, introduced me to the art of eating winkles and jellied eels and generally acted as my mentor. She wore a pair of purple suede, zip-up boots, with stacked soles, and a pewter-coloured herringbone tweed suit with a tiny waistcoat, while I had a trouser suit by Ossie Clarke which was fitted at the waist and had flared trousers. Running out of money towards the end of term, I frequently made my own skirts and trousers from pieces of furnishing fabric that were purchased from John Lewis. There were complaints from members of staff at the college as well as schools I visited, about the length of these skirts. I had an Indian top I was very proud of, which was cream cotton with flared sleeves and embroidery around the hem, neck and cuffs. It came to just below my bottom. With the lace-up thong sandals I had bought in Greece and my brown legs and long hair, I felt I was an object of admiration in the local pub when I went home, though I was probably more an object of lust and amusement. My mother pointedly refused to comment on my appearance, but it was clear she disapproved. My sister invariably dressed in black and maintained the image of tragedy queen. She rarely opened her mouth to smile, but concentrated on making up her eyes and keeping disdainfully aloof from me and my friends, who, it had to be said, were a rather motley bunch. She went to art college and did well, but none of the joyousness and carefree lifestyle I enjoyed for much of the time seemed to rub off on her. She came to my parties but complained that no one spoke to her, and that she found teachers and their friends boring and small minded.

While understanding this to some extent, I recognised that here was my mother's influence at work. The idea of letting her hair down and enjoying herself for once was anathema to her then. For my brother, then fifteen, it was unthinkable. It's possible he never forgave me (and later my sister) for moving out and leaving him with our parents. There were escape routes open to him later, as we got our own places and he could have stayed or even moved in, but he never once visited any place I ever lived in, though he was frequently invited. He accepted his fate stoically, while blaming me for it. For a while he retained a sense of humour, linked to the odd and the unexpected, and had a collection of bizarre and amusing videos that he would bring out to show us if we visited him. My sister found very little to amuse her.

"There's not much to smile about," she would say. "I don't find there's much to laugh at."

My father could still laugh, when the mood took him; so could my mother, when presented with some absurdity or amusing incident. But they rarely laughed at things together, unless I was at home and had their attention. In telling a funny story, I would have to direct myself to her, so that she could hear me, and he would feel left out, though I tried to include him. She would be distracted by his laughter and glance at him to see if he was sharing the joke, but he rarely responded to her with a look or a comment to indicate he had heard. They were not to be united, even by a joke, it seemed. The attention was on me, never each other, and my yearning to unite them, and free my brother and sister from the tyranny of this parental stalemate, was always to be thwarted. My brother and sister never attempted to make any unity between them; they must have realised such attempts were doomed.

It was at a concert at Farnborough Tech that I first noticed Sam. With wild red hair and a pale, acne scarred face, on top of a beach weakling's body, he was not what anyone would call attractive, but he had women flocking around him. I was curious. Dancing with him, it became clear that he liked women and was interested in them as people. This was a novelty to me in some ways, coming from a family such as mine, but Sam had a very direct way of getting to the heart of things, and self-deprecation was one way he had of diverting you from his looks. He had just ended a difficult affair with a woman whose docker father threatened to kill both of them. Eventually he backed off. Highly intelligent, but aware that he came from a different background to that of his girlfriend, he reluctantly stopped seeing her. We talked and became close. Gradually our relationship became the most important thing in my life. He understood about my parents; he was having a hard time with his, and he had decided on a change of career, so that instead of following his father into the engineering business he had developed in Scotland, and being bribed with expensive gifts—a TR4—he had decided to change direction completely and study psychology. We spent three passionate years together before it came to an end, but in that time, he became another bridge from my family to the outside world, and taught me to trust in myself. Together we heard Dylan at the Albert Hall, Bert Jansch, The Incredible String Band, went to peace marches, festivals and poetry readings and shared books, music and a love of Leonard Cohen.

NINETEEN

It's nineteen sixty-seven and my sister has a boyfriend, Jake, an ex-merchant seaman who at twenty-two is now going to art college and turning his hand to all sorts of projects to get by financially. The eldest of four brothers, he is very good-looking, amusing, and annoying, and prides himself on being a bit of a wild man. But he is very talented and he seems very keen on Janet. He enjoys provoking people, especially my parents. After he falls out with Janet, he marries a Spanish painter and becomes quite famous. We keep in touch with him, but my mother doesn't know this.

My mother hates him. During the summer of '67, Steven is away in America and I am at home with my parents, working as a scullery hand for a geriatric hospital. There's a rumour of a beach party at Littlehampton, on the sand dunes, and we decide to go.

Jake's brother has a car, we find another from a friend of his, a man none of us knows, and a large group of us set off for the coast on a Saturday afternoon in these two cars, packed in like sardines. Littlehampton in the early evening is full of young men selling purple hearts and weak cannabis, and Jake buys some stuff, to Janet's annoyance, and we head for the beach. Someone is setting up a barbeque. There are hairy young men with guitars trying out chords, but no sign of the crowds we had expected. It's early, and we buy chips in town and wander about, waiting for things to start. Then a thunderstorm blows up and fills the horizon with pewter billows, from which slashes of pure white lightening emerge, getter closer until we are forced to shelter in the cars. It does not blow over. Rain comes down in torrents, but inside the cars we laugh and smoke the cannabis and fall asleep eventually. One couple have brought a tent that they erect on the golf course, to the cheers of the onlookers. The barbeque has been abandoned and there are disconsolate dripping wet young people huddled under bushes and in bus shelters, where they have to spend the night. We find a fourteen year old in a bus shelter the next morning and give him a lift home. We enjoy ourselves hugely even though the party and the band never materialise.

    I felt a part of the exuberance of youth. I had found another family to belong to; one that did not recognise the barriers of class, nationality or social status and it was good. The year before this, I had had a fleeting affair with a young man who had travelled to Israel, alone, after a row with his parents, working his way round the Mediterranean, and whose thirst for continued travel matched my own. Together we had hitchhiked to Greece, slept in Swiss hotel grounds, under a bamboo hedge, roughed it again in Germany, sleeping in a bus station at Ulm, and finally arrived in the Greek island of Poros, sleeping on a beach by a disused well swarming with hornets, under the eucalyptus trees. We swam at night in the dark waters of the bay, amid phosphorus that trailed silvery strings of droplets down our bodies when we came out. Although I didn't love him, and it was very much a relationship of convenience, he taught me again to trust the world and myself. We met young German couples sheltering on the autobahn under the bridges, talked to French and Italian youths who were travelling with difficulty through Yugoslavia, met American draft dodgers desperate not to take part in the Vietnam War, exchanged information and food, cigarettes and yarns, and felt, despite being unwashed, tired and often hungry, very pleased with our lives. The young who travelled in the Sixties had only one thing in common, a desire to escape and explore. It was a multi-racial, classless society, not composed as it is now of students and the moneyed young, but of young workers, idealists and drifters. Most had no money, but needed little. They worked as they went, scrounged what they could, shared what they had and settled for minimum standards of hygiene, food and shelter. It was a community. We read Kerouac, Ginsberg and Ferlinghetti and dreamed of the road, we read *Soledad Brother*, James Baldwin and Frantz Fanon and dreamed of a world where people could be equal;

we read Genet and Sartre and discovered new worlds of thought and experience. We wanted our thinking to be challenged and we were ready to do some challenging ourselves. The student revolts of '68 had almost arrived.

Back at college, I became interested again in writing poetry and Alan Brownjohn encouraged me. We went to poetry readings and I had some work published. I became established with Steve; gradually he opted in more and more in our relationship and I recognised the similarities between his home and mine. He had as well as the older brother who was blind, and an Oxford undergraduate, a younger brother who was on the point of leaving home. He was close to them both. His father, a gentle, mild-mannered man, was charming; his mother quite formidable. He was close to his father, but not his mother. But the difference was that no one was expected to take sides, and his parents had a good social life and went on holiday together in a way that was unthinkable for my parents. We travelled around Europe together and became one another's close companions. I had finally settled down.

Eight years further on and we are leaving London. Steve has got a job as deputy head of a Special School in Lancashire and we are moving. I know no one up there but feel that our two children will benefit by being out of London. My mother is cross and says so. Surely we could have found work nearer home? She means by this her home. We had tried, to be fair, to find work in the South, but the cost of housing in Hampshire at that time was higher than Hackney, and although we had several interviews between us, nothing came of them. Steve's mother, who has just been widowed, wishes us well. Steve grieves for his father. He is only twenty-eight and losing his father has been a terrible shock. I have lost my cousin, dead at twenty-nine from melanoma, just after the birth of our first son. Welcoming the new baby and regretting the loss of my cousin so bitterly is an exhausting mental exercise. Somehow we have each other and survive. My sister is shocked and devastated by this loss. Newly married, his wife and friends were her escape route and survival kit, and when he died, the hopes of the whole family died with him. An only child of elderly adoring parents, he had not had time to provide a grandchild to leave as a legacy. His courteous, optimistic and good-humoured personality was gone and nothing could replace it. I had a need to protect our son from so much suffering. Because he was only three weeks old and I was still so sore and breastfeeding him, it was impossible to go to the funeral. This was a constant sadness afterwards, because it separated me from my sister and brother even more. But the new life needed me more, and needed me intact to deal with it. By this time Janet's relationship with Jake had ended; he was too much the wild man and the drugs had got out of hand. My mother was pleased. My sister, now nearly thirty, had no one.

I go back to work, teaching in Hackney. Our first son is nine months old when I wean him. I am immediately pregnant again, despite having a coil. I am shocked and terrified of another pregnancy. I cannot contemplate another hospital confinement. The pain and uncaring treatment I received first time around, which ended only with a forceps delivery and terrible bruising, and Steve put out of the room, was not going to be my lot this time around, I vowed. Neither would my baby be separated from me after his birth as Rob had been. I find a doctor who reluctantly agrees to attend a home delivery for me, provided the baby is on time. On the night of Harry's birth, we have friends round for supper and I drink some castor oil mixed with neat squash and baking soda. Shortly after one o'clock in the morning he is born, eyes wide open, into the arms of his father and the elderly midwife, Sister Licorish. It is a very different occasion. He is a beautiful baby and his brother hates him for the first six months of his life. My mother tries to be supportive, and offers practical help in the form of gifts of a pushchair and clothing. I am exhausted and sleep whenever I can during that year.

The year before we leave London is tiring too. Steve needs a certificate in Special Education from Goldsmiths before he can get promotion. He gives up his job in a school for what are then termed maladjusted children, and I work full time to support us. I cash in my pension to help pay for his course. At weekends he has a shellfish round in the East End, selling cockles and whelks to the punters in the pubs. Midweek he has a half-day off and takes on a night job, cleaning the Underground. Besides teaching, I work in an adult education centre one night a week. Between us, we have five different jobs. The children are juggled between us, and a willing friend, and we all survive. But it's been hard. We can work as a team, know how to find work, are able to survive on little money. I go to the West Indian butchers in Dalston and get pigs' feet, chopped lamb for curry, learn to make rice and peas, peanut chop, red beans with coconut. Ridley Road market is where I push the double pushchair on Fridays to fetch the vegetables. Bread from Kossoff's and bread pudding, cut in thick slabs and flavoured with cinnamon and sultanas, keeps the children quiet in their pram while I haggle with the costermongers for fish and bananas. On the way home, I stop at the eel and mash shop and the boys admire the slippery eels in the porcelain container outside the shop. I cook vegetable soups, pasta, beans and lentils. I learn from my neighbours, our friends and our lodgers. I eat things I've never seen before, pickled pigs trotters, spicy and savoury, dasheen, plantain, sweet potato, snapper fish, okra. There is always someone living with us in London, someone who needs a small room with a bed and someone to talk to. We need the rent. We are all young, all needy, but it's fun. My mother doesn't approve.

"Caroline, there's a black man in your bathroom. Did you know?"

"Yes, Mum, it's M'bye. He's lodging with us. He's a student but his government won't pay his fees, so he's staying with us for a week or two." I didn't add that this man had a German common law wife and had lived with her and their child in a room smaller than the dining room at Somersets, until they ran out of money. M'bye was a man of some standing back home in the Gambia, a handsome, hardworking man who hoped to go back and get a job in the Government when he had gained his economics degree. It was from him that I learned to cook the African dish known as peanut chop. London was full of people like him, hopeful and eager to learn. His wife had gone back to Germany with their child, a confused little bundle who clung to his mother. Life was tough. My mother had no idea about the lives of other people, but did her best, and her natural good manners made it impossible for her to be anything but pleasant to the motley assortment of people who shared our lives.

"Well, I don't know," was often her concluding remark. There was a strong sense of community among the people of Hackney then; it was a real melting pot, for race, political conviction, class and religion. No one group predominated.

My mother hated us living there; it wasn't what she had in mind for me at all; it was the dirt and crowds she disliked rather than the place itself, but my father quite enjoyed the liveliness of the place and offered practical help with some of the building work we undertook. My mother was forced to acknowledge that other people may look different, come from a different place and have different customs, but essentially we all experience the same problems. This helped her to become less paranoid for a while. She softened her racist attitudes a little by contact with the very minorities she had previously railed against.

Our house was a tiny terrace, in Stoke Newington, and we bought it, knowing we would have to leave our rented flat now that a baby was on the way. It was almost the cheapest house for sale anywhere in London. It had been a boarding house, and there were curry stains on the walls, junk all over the garden and each room had a padlock on it. We set to work on it with a will. Hugely pregnant, once I had given up my teaching post, I got to work with a blowtorch killing the dry rot spores in the kitchen extension and chipping off rotten plaster, while Steve became an overnight bricklayer, tiler and plasterer. Our neighbours, who didn't know us well, were very welcoming and offered all kinds of help.

Friends came up and stayed and painted the baby's room a lurid shade of yellow, which had to be changed the moment they left, as it was too violent a colour even for me. We were happy, despite our poverty.

Just after Harry was born, Kate came into our lives. Seventeen, she had a job working in St. James Park, as a gardener. Her parents had thrown her out for insubordination and not tidying her bedroom and she had nowhere to stay. A mutual friend introduced us. Kate was highly intelligent and a born rebel, used to standing her ground and arguing the toss with anyone, including us. But she was great. Long, dark hair framed a round face with a sweet smile, marked by a broken front tooth, which she had capped with gold. She was robust and strong and wore donkey jackets and jeans. She came into our kitchen and sat heavily in the grandfather chair and introduced herself. After a while, she said, "Will I do?" in a little girl's voice, and my heart went out to her. She would more than do; she would be great. And she was. She had tried very hard to be the daughter her mother wanted her to be, but she was more like her father in appearance, and her parents had parted years before. Her stepfather, whom she adored, was unable to mend the rift between mother and daughter. There was a fellow feeling here all right, with this plainly dressed, plain speaking, assertive young women. She was sensible, good humoured and patient with the boys, who took to her immediately as she taught them the Cockney alphabet, amused them with jokes and stories, and bathed their grazes. None of this was in her rent agreement, but she offered it willingly. A friend commented that she looked like a female dustman, but that they'd like to have her beside them in a fight. I couldn't have put it better myself.

Because we had a number of people lodging with us from time to time, and they happened to be Communists, or had connections with the Communist Party, working for the Morning Star, our telephone became tapped and our post began to arrive already opened and clumsily resealed. An IRA bomb factory was found in Evering Road, close to our house, and we noted the coincidence—Lavender Hill, Clapham Northside—there had been bomb factories here too, near our flats. They appeared to be following us around London. No wonder our post was opened. We were not members of the Communist Party—it had been difficult for me to separate myself from my religious beliefs as a teenager and I was not about to take up another religion, one moreover that would demand even more of me. Even talking to Kay Beauchamp and Tony Gilbert, two Spanish Civil War veterans, didn't entirely convince me that the Communist Party had all the answers. I knew many other political activists in Hackney in those days and their lives were not an example I wanted to follow. Some lived in squalor, self-chosen, as a way of showing solidarity with the oppressed of the world, many sacrificed their partners and children to their principles, then left them and went off with a campadre who was unfettered by children. It was an incestuous community and there were many casualties as people changed partners, sabotaged community projects and traded political insults. The ideology of the left was a great deal more fluid and open to debate than that of the far right. The Nazi Party and Moseley's brown shirts were still alive in the memories of older people in the area, who had chased them out of the East End in Cable Street, although they still had a headquarters in Brick Lane. Nazi and National Front ideology seemed to be simple and direct— kill, evict or drive out all those identified as non-white. The Front did not appear to expend the same amount of energy fighting one another that the far left did, although maybe it was just because we didn't get to hear about the divisions, while the C.P. took little trouble to hide its rifts and with its myriad of factions and tendencies, there was always an opportunity for the anarchists to foul things up, or the Socialist Workers to get out of hand.

London became dangerous to move around in. Oxford Street and the West End were subjected to IRA car bombs on a weekly basis and hoaxes were commonplace. Irish people kept to their own areas as the suspicion and tension in the community mounted. Rubbish bins vanished from stations and some public places. There were some rules normally adhered to—the bombs were mostly at weekends in the West End, there were usually few casualties, and due warning was given. But there were exceptions, and copycat bombings happened, which did enormous damage and there were enough casualties to make everyone nervous.

Some of the National Front activity also threatened our normal friendships with people in our area, but at the same time it also cemented some other relationships, as people found their beliefs tested. Meena, a beautiful young Indian mother of two boys who lived at the end of our street was in tears. Her husband explained that she was being followed on a daily basis, by a man who shouted insults at her and exposed himself. She was frightened to take her boys to school. I supported her through the ordeal of giving evidence to the police, and in return, was invited to a family feast. These exchanges were and are commonplace in multi-cultural areas and for my mother, it was all something of an eye opener. The community looked after itself, and included us in that. Random acts of kindness, from people warning us when our car was about to be broken into, to free help with our kitchen in exchange for advice about dealing with a difficult child, came our way often. We gave what we had to others and found that, in general, the world gave us back all sorts of unexpected treasures.

Living in a squalid rented house along the road from us was a family of travellers who ran a scrap metal and rag-and-bone business, though they described themselves as totters. They had a profoundly deaf son, who was usually away at boarding school but at home in the holidays. Robert, the son, was given to car breaking in the road outside our house on summer evenings, an activity involving a sledgehammer and an awful lot of noise, which he was unable to hear. His father found him difficult to control and the neighbours, including us, wanted Robert to stop smashing vehicles to pieces during the night. Taking an interest in him proved to be the best thing we could do. Robert was also an excellent carver and with a bit of encouragement made us a carved wooden stork, which we still have. This became his activity of choice, encouraged by his school, and the nighttime noise abated. His father, George, used to pop by at intervals after this with strange items he'd come across and which he felt might interest us. I came by a nice Spode dish that way and a copper World War One canteen. We paid George a nominal sum for these items, knowing he could have sold them for more, but honoured to receive them. It was in this way that we began a lifetime of collecting items that had seen better days and other uses. Along with most of our friends, we had little in the house that was new. We had no television, no washing machine, and no car. I wheeled the washing to the public laundry during the evening, in the pram. Our table was a cable holder, painted red and on its side, a gigantic bobbin stable enough to hold potted plants and a few toys. The best toys our little boys had were cardboard boxes, painted and made into miniature cookers, cupboards, post boxes, tables and beds for stuffed animals.

They were very inventive with these and with their collections of toy cars and wooden railway wagons. A sheet hung over the kitchen table became a den into which little rabbits ran when the wolf approached, a game they never tired of. Their way of getting to bed was their father shouting 'Horsie! The horse is going upstairs!' as two excited and tired little boys climbed onto their father's back and set off up the stairs. The treasures we had were our few possessions and each other. It was a happy house.

TWENTY

When we've been settled in our new house in Lancashire for a while my parents come up and see us. They approve of the house, more or less. We sit down and I tell them our news.

"We've got something to tell you, haven't we, Steve?" He nods. "We're going to have another baby. I'm about three months pregnant." My mother looks aghast.

"Oh, Caroline, how could you? You must be mad. Haven't you got enough on your plate?" My father keeps quiet, scared to say anything. Steve says that now we're more comfortably off and have a bigger house, we've decided to have this baby. It wasn't an accident, he implies; we meant it to happen.

I am wounded to the core. She has done it again, thrown cold water and condemnation over everything I hold dear. How rude of her! How dare she! I am speechless with rage and indignation. The visit does not go well. She comes to visit when the baby's born, but I don't want her there. Forgiveness is slow to come. Later, she does it again when our foster son joins our family. This happens rather by accident.

The family at the end of our terrace are in difficulties. They have six children between them, four girls and two boys, from their previous marriages. The children are treated harshly and the mother has mental health problems. One of the boys is always in trouble and makes our home his refuge. He runs away from home often and the police, who bring him back, talk to the social services about him. We are approached to see if we could offer this young man a temporary home, where he could continue to have contact with his family, but be out of the spotlight for a while. We agree, and Mark spends the next few weeks curled in a foetal position in front of our fire, sucking his thumb. He is quiet and obedient, not that we ask much from him, reasoning that what he needs is shelter. We go through a vetting process in this time. After three weeks he returns home, and we write a letter to say that in our opinion he should not be forced to live at home if he does not want to be there. After more trouble, he is removed and placed in a children's home, where we keep some contact with him. Now our names are on the list, and we hope to offer a permanent home to a needy child. There's a four-year gap between our youngest and middle son and we feel another child would slot in here without too much trouble. It doesn't work out like this. One Friday evening the social worker contacts us. She has a young man on her doorstep who has left the family he has been with and needs shelter. He is sixteen, much older than our children. He can't go to a children's home because the staff are on strike and not taking new admissions. Can we have him for the weekend until other arrangements can be made? Of course we agree, and a serious, slender, dark-haired young man arrives on our doorstep half an hour later. We spend time talking to him, asking him about himself. He had not long left school and had an apprenticeship that he was forced to give up, as his foster parents wanted him to do A Levels. He was unhappy at this. He had a row with them one night about homework and walked out. The family seems to have been under some stress at this time and quite possibly were glad he had left, reducing the number of teenagers in the house to four. They did not keep in touch, though he made contact with them. He found a job immediately and stayed with us for the next seven years, at our invitation, then moved into his own flat nearby. Although everything we knew and had been told about him said he was a straight, sober and honest person, my parents were not happy.

"You're clutching a serpent to your bosom," said my father dramatically.

My mother was extremely displeased, even though in her own family, there was a history of accommodating strangers. She herself had been given a home by her aunt. Perhaps the lack of a blood connection made it difficult for her to trust someone from outside.

Knowing he wasn't welcome made visits difficult and I kicked myself for not realising that their attitude would cause problems. We hadn't had time to prepare ourselves, never mind them, for having him around. Steven's mother was more willing to offer the hand of friendship, but then she wasn't deaf and mixed more in society generally. Sean was to be a great source of support and help to our family in many ways over the following years and my father said eventually that he was a credit to us and we had done well in caring for him. Knowing that the truth was rather different, I swallowed and accepted the compliment. I don't think of myself as special in that way anyway, sometimes fate hands us something and we deal with it as best we may.

It's hard not having a mother around. She comes like a shot when there's a disaster, but she isn't interested when things are going well, and I need her to be. The new baby is a delight and I don't have to rush back to work this time, I can stay and be a proper mother to our three little boys.

When the baby became a sturdy, blond toddler with an angelic smile, we arranged a holiday in Scotland for my mother, and mother-in-law Maggie was to come too. I left it up to my mother whether she invited my father along, but made it clear he would be welcome, though the holiday was for her. He drove them both up and we all set off for Kirkcudbright the next day. The cottage we hired was pleasant and the scenery exactly how my mother had imagined it. She had wanted all her life to go to Scotland, and now she was there. I hoped she'd enjoy the trip. She spent the evening of our arrival apologising to Maggie for my father:

"He *is* odd. Honestly, I despair." Clearly he embarrassed her a great deal. Maggie remained unruffled and talked to both of them equally. We looked at the loch, and the mountains in the distance. The next morning a man on a motor-bike zoomed up to the house with a message. My grandmother, Bill, had had a stroke and was not expected to live. It had to happen. My mother's belief: that if you leave home, awful things happen, has caused the curse to work again. And it's *his* mother, of course, awkward as always, spoiling her holiday by dying. My father feels it's his fault, and they get back into the car and trundle south again. We are not expected to go to the funeral.

Later, they come up again and appear to have some sort of truce this time. They walk round a small town carnival and hold hands, something I've never seen before. Our friends come round and play music on the lawn and my mother admires my friend's new baby. I have a photo of them both sitting side by side in the sunshine, looking, for once, contented.

Their golden wedding comes around and I try to involve my brother and sister in some recognition of this.

"Call it a marriage? There's nothing to celebrate." My sister snorts and offers no support.

"It's their marriage. It might not look good to you or me, but it is their marriage." Silence follows and in the end, I arrange for flowers and champagne to be sent along with a card from all of us. My mother thanks me, guardedly. My father takes them both out for a meal, but it falls flat.

"I don't think she enjoyed it much," he says to me on the phone later. Had she expected a present? If so, he failed there. And he would have taken her to a pub where he knows the landlord, having repaired his central heating boiler, rather than a restaurant serving the sort of food she likes. Everything has always been on his terms, I think. She won't tell him what she wants because he always disregards it.

Why, I think, do my brother and sister need to keep between the two of them? Whether we like it or not, they are a couple who have chosen to stay together. Yet, they're not given the chance to have any kind of a relationship, without the scorn of my sister or the distress of my brother. My father is a bully, we all agree on that, and exhausting to deal with. But he has never hit her, very seldom has he hit us: neither of them believed that it was the way the way to raise children, but without my mother there as a brake, he might have been very different. Instead, he uses knowledge and his tongue to browbeat others, on a daily basis. I can see that she has run out of energy. She wants to switch off from him and be left alone in her silent world, where she doesn't have to answer his silly questions or listen to his feeble jokes, or respond to his negative comments about her. He doesn't learn from his mistakes. And the reason he doesn't learn is because he doesn't listen, because if he did, he would have to acknowledge that someone else was telling him things he didn't want to hear or know, and that other people have feelings too.

I never quite give up, but when he bullies me, or tries the manipulative trick of threatening suicide once again, I now hand the responsibility back to him very firmly. But he still has me in tears from time to time, as she does.

Her bitterness increases as her realisation of being trapped in this angry, upset family increases. She loves us all in her own way, except my father, but she also hates us for not being able to rescue her from her life, especially my father. He felt he had rescued her when he married her; who else would have married poor deaf little Edith? She had no one else. And he knows he made her happy by giving her children. Is that enough? It has to be; he will get no more.

Love without freedom is a terrifying thing. Without freedom, we are tied to the one who claims to love us for the whole of our lives. How can we fight them? How can we get away from them? Vulnerability keeps them tied to us, and us to them.

I never thought that my parents were as vulnerable, especially my mother, as my brother and sister did. I knew that my mother could have done many things with her life, had many qualities that were never explored. I knew my father had held her back by belittling her skills. I knew my parents had it in them to renew their relationship, or end it, once their children had left them. But they never did leave, and the terrible stalemate carried on and on. It was too easy to use us as referees, comforters, adjudicators and shields against the other. Without us, they would fall apart. This was the myth we bought. We were the parents, they the children.

When at nineteen, I contemplate leaving the family for good I have terrible nightmares. It is night-time, and the house (which is isolated) seems even more lonely. Danger lurks outside. A crazy man with an axe is trying to attack the family; he wants to break in and destroy everything. I'm not sure the other family members are aware of this. But I know. I know I have to get out of the house and make a run for it, to get help. But I can't leave the house. Who will protect them if I'm not there? Yet if I don't leave, we're all doomed anyway. Sweating, I wake up. The dream stays with me. It reappears in different forms every few nights. Can I go? By staying, I would relinquish my right to adulthood, sanity and relationships outside the house. By going, I would abandon them to their fate. Could they cope without me to hold the balance?

Actually, nothing much changed. My mother reserved her most vitriolic comments about my father for me whenever we met; my father still used me as an emotional leaning post. My mother never forgave me for leaving her and waited for some awful fate to befall me, as it had her. I dealt with the guilt of this by writing cheerful, optimistic letters to her, and writing open letters to them both.

My mother's letters became by degrees more and more gloomy and laden with anxiety.

Dear Caroline,

How is work going? I do hope you're not overdoing things; glandular fever can be very nasty. Your cousin had it and it took him ages to feel right again. I had to take Douglas to the doctor's last week with a bad chest. The doctors down there are useless. He seems a little better today. Mrs. B next door has been ill. I went to see her in the hospital and she looks awful, poor thing. Do be careful in London. You hear such awful stories about girls being abducted and taken away. You will be careful, won't you? By the way, I saw Joanne yesterday. She's expecting a baby and her mother is furious. She doesn't know who the father is. I don't know what the world's coming to. Father's putting a new roof on the shed at last. I have packed up the clothes you left behind here and will send them to you when I have time. I hope they arrive safely; the local postman has been prosecuted for theft. I always thought there was something strange about him. You can't trust anyone these days. No news really, just jogging along.

Well, must go now and start the ironing.
Love,
Mum.

Sometimes, the letter would lie like an unexploded bomb on my hall carpet, waiting for me to open it so that the anger and grief of all the trivial awfulness of her life could burst out and infect me with its misery. Only years later when someone pointed out to me that it was unfair for her to continually dump all this on me, did I stop to think about it. Was it possible for her to write about the pleasant, happy, non-troubling things in her life? It wasn't; it never occurred to her and it never happened.

She continually confused my life with hers and expected my life to be as difficult as hers had been. My father's letters were, as expected, rambling missives about his past life and loves. Neither parent was able to respond to my letters or my real concerns. In fact, I dare not tell my mother about the things that really upset me, knowing they would be seized upon and used to add further detail to the gloomy picture of the world she already possessed. I decided that some families are like vultures; they hover around when there's a death or a disaster, but they're not interested when the intended victim is alive and kicking. Our family never celebrated. Only dependency and vulnerability were given credence. Maybe there was nothing to celebrate from their point of view, and certainly there was a lot to be glum about, but I found this attitude hard to accept. There are no birthday parties after we grow up, no family celebrations. We meet other distant family members at funerals. The fun of family life has never been there for my family and more and more I grieve for the brother and sister I might have had, the in-laws, the nephews and nieces. I am one of only two members of my generation out of nine who have children. Three of the others are dead. It feels lonely. I dream of the daughter my sister might have had, an auburn-haired, brown-eyed child, and sigh. I love my boys, but had hoped for a daughter as well.

As I have my own children and they bring me immense pleasure, I long to share this with Douglas, Janet and my parents. I have a sense of guilt about having left them. I have a sense of not deserving my happiness and freedom. These take time to dispel. I create my own, happier family, and surround myself with them. My mother gives my sister things, either trying to make up for her unhappiness or as a bribe to get her to stay, I can't decide.

TWENTY-ONE

I have a treasure. I have a memory of a day spent in London with my mother, who, free from the influences of the house and family, enjoyed herself enormously. She had come on her own, a brave gesture on her part, and I had come down from Lancashire, leaving the children with their father for the day. We met at Covent Garden and had a wonderful day together visiting the automaton museum and watching the buskers and street performers. She was relaxed, despite her dislike of London, and over lunch we talked, joked, and laughed together as women and as equals. It never happened before or since, but she was a different woman without the rest of the family around her, and I treasure the memory. I know she did too.

Things were easier between us after this. I wondered how this kind of experience could ever happen with my father and brother, or my sister and my mother. Although it was late in the day when my sister moved out, she was able to establish herself as an independent separate person to some extent.

When she finally moves out of Somersets, following a row with my father and then me, when I tell her I don't know why she is still there at all at the age of forty, she worries about the family treasures left behind, which she feels my mother is unable to look after. She sets up her new little home, adding some treasures to her collection of furniture and knick-knacks.

Soon her little house is full and bursting at the seams. I am uneasy about this, as our mother doesn't know what is missing. Two years before her death I visit my parents with our oldest son, who has just returned from a work stint abroad, and my mother remembers she has something she wants to give him. She goes upstairs and rummages about, coming down with a large old sketch-book, beautifully illustrated by my Great-Uncle Felix. I have never seen this book before. The book is a travel journal of the part of the world my son has just visited—Israel, Jordan and what was then Palestine. She wants him to have it. He is excited by this book, as he was when she showed him her other treasure, a small parchment bound book from the 17th Century of recipes and simples handed down through the family from generation to generation. We both love this little book; it's precious because of the everyday nature of the simples and the connection with our family. To cure an arrow wound the book recommended, 'take hog's dung hot from the hog and lay it to the wound.' Rob, who loved books from the time he first had one read to him, was enchanted by the age and history of the book.

Recognising from Felix's book some of the views he had illustrated, from his own travels, he spent a happy half hour telling his grandmother about his trip and the places he had visited that coincided with the book illustrations.

There are three or four other books written by Felix that should be in the house, illustrating his honeymoon with Great-Aunt Ethel and their grand tour of Europe in a coach and four. These are whimsical and amusing, but they have disappeared from the house and my mother searches in vain for them, wanting to give them to us along with the bigger sketchbook. She apologises for not finding them. I think I know where they are.

My father's books have disappeared too, old handpainted volumes of flower paintings painted by one of his mother's forbears. They are exquisite volumes, and very valuable. My sister doesn't know they belong to my father, and as she sees it, they are falling apart and in need of restoration. She pays to have them rebound. My father has no idea she has them; maybe she wouldn't have taken them if she had known they belonged to him, such is her antipathy towards him. He is pleased that they have been restored and as she now has them in her possession, he decides not to ask for them back.

He gets to know later who owns them when he is given a paper to sign saying that they now belong to her. It seems she cannot be challenged. I am, I realise, scared of upsetting her, just as my mother is. She looms over me, almost six feet tall in her shoes, and her eyes, which never settle, seem always ready to brim over and spill down her angry face. She has put on weight and her double chins give her the appearance of a large frightened baby. I don't know how to approach her.

Mother is dying. She has been talking about it for a long time, waiting for it to happen. She has had a bad pain in her abdomen but the doctor says it's nothing. However, it's a burst abscess and her blood pressure is so low they can't operate when they do get her into hospital. She has septicaemia and has lost a lot of blood. She is seventy-eight and still looks quite robust. She lapses into a coma. Surely she can't be about to die? She lies in intensive care for days, hovering between life and death and we sit with her, my sister and I, while our father and brother come and go. A drip goes into a Malibu container on the floor, which I find incongruous. My mother never tasted Malibu in her life, would only have sherry at Christmas under pressure. Cook's perks, she would say, handing me a glass. She spreads her large, strong freckled brown hands on the white sheet, oblivious to the world and our tears. I try and comfort our father, but he cannot believe she is so ill. The nurses talk about switching off the life support machine, but decide to give her a few more days, as she seems to be rallying a little. We keep vigil beside her bed.

Eventually she regains consciousness little by little, but is not pleased to be back with the living, blaming us for the fact that she is still alive. We've robbed her, or somebody has, of her desired end, death. She has a colostomy, which she hates, and her body is sore with the mass of injection sites and tubes that enter and leave her like motorways from a city centre. My sister and I are exhausted. My father is quietly triumphant—he told us she wouldn't die and he's been proved right. We don't have the energy to hate him for this. I go back to my family and my work. I can take no more leave.

Her slow recovery, which might have given the family a second chance, changes nothing. She is even more bitter towards my father, switching her hearing aid off when he enters the ward and closing her eyes, blaming him for the fact that she is still alive. Their conversations, if they have any, are private, but with us she maintains her hostility towards him.

She becomes paranoid at times, suspecting everyone of conspiring against her. This is a hazard the deaf face, I am told, and the only way I can deal with it is to challenge the more florid and irrational thoughts. It's been there on and off throughout her life, I realise, but it's very marked in her later years. She moans at me.

"I wish I had some help in the house."

"I'll talk to Dad and ask him to find somebody."

"No, it's all right. I don't want anyone from the village."

"Oh?"

"You can't trust any of them. Thieves and liars. Wouldn't trust one of them. Ask anybody."

"What all of them? Even Marge?" Marge was the last helper who gave up to nurse her sick husband. "Even Mrs. Chitty and Mrs. Robinson?"

"Oh, Marge was all right."

"So they're not all bad then?" She glares at me. I have caught her out and she doesn't like it. But she gets a cleaner who is recommended by a friend.

Two years later, she has breast cancer and another operation. The colostomy is reversed and the lump in her breast is taken away. She is surprisingly sanguine about this, but when it becomes clear that she will endure this too and still not die, she returns home, where she has almost become a prisoner, and becomes more depressed, more slow and more unable to function until bit by bit all her faculties begin to fail. She still beats me at scrabble, and can do a crossword, but she is most alive when anger surfaces, and as usual this is with my father, though never to his face. Afraid to attack him, when he cares for her in many practical ways, she attacks me instead. She reserves the vitriol for me, hoping I'll deliver it to him and is angry when I can't, or don't or won't. I can't play the go-between or the message carrier anymore and I tell her gently she should give her own messages to him. But she won't. He does her washing, washes up, cleans the bathroom, pays her bills, cooks a meal, mends things that break, takes her shopping and to the doctor and dentist when she can no longer see to drive. He gets no thanks for any of this. Then she gets really ill again with what the doctor thinks is a stroke. The consultant doesn't read her notes when she is admitted and assumes that when she does not respond to his questions and instructions to move her feet and hands, that she has had a stroke so severe that she is unable to do anything.

We explain, patiently, that she is deaf and has to be approached in such a way so that she can see the speaker's face and hear what is being said to her. We have to explain this over and over again to the nurses, auxiliaries and others who attend to her. She becomes dehydrated because there is no one to watch her drink and her eyes have become so weak that she can't see when a drink is being put down. The ward is full of dying elderly women, all needing attention at times, some demented, some incontinent, some ghostly pale and lying very still, but able to hear every word.

There are no staff in the ward; they sit out in the corridor at a desk that overlooks three such wards and they cannot be seen by the patients, nor can the staff see them with any ease. Every patient has an alarm that they can press, but most, including our mother, are so weak or disorientated that finding and reaching it in an emergency is a real problem. Somehow my mother breaks her arm and it is never explained how she has done this. Somehow the demented but sweet natured lady in the next bed manages to hurt her legs by falling over obstacles, and dies of pneumonia after a bad fall, going from able-bodied to comatose in three weeks. No one is around to hear or see them.

My mother now has a diagnosis. She has a brain tumour. Whether this is related to her past breast cancer, for which she had the all-clear just before she became ill again, we are not told, and it's not important. They can't operate. She doesn't, in any case, want them to. Finally she is going to die and she is in someway excited at the prospect. There's something more noble sounding about having a brain tumour than a stroke or Alzheimer's; it has more class. Dehydration plays tricks on her brain when she is first brought in to the hospital and she imagines she's in a French Resistance movie. If we could sneak her past the guards, she could make a run for it. The Gestapo are waiting round the corner; we would have to disguise ourselves to smuggle her out. Amid our tears the incongruity of her fantasies and hallucinations, which cheer her up, also cheer us too; in a grotesque way, they almost make her illness bearable at this point.

The visual hallucinations, caused in part by her medication, in part her dehydration, became quite florid.

"I say, Caroline, what's that parrot doing up there?" She points, squinting, at the curtain rail. The multicoloured macaw perches on her bed rail. It walks back and forth, squawking and nodding its head up and down. She can't believe it's not really there and her description is so vivid, we too can picture this gorgeous bird strutting above our heads. It is sad to tell her it isn't real. Then she sees a cat on the next bed, and the nurses become wicked little aliens, out to hurt her. She talks loudly about the doctors, especially one who has given her an injection.

"Just a little prick," she keeps saying, over and over, in a voice that carries way beyond the bed. "It was just a little prick," as we veer between hysteria and alarm.

"Don't tell everyone," we say finally, to quieten her. She is not familiar with the pejorative use of the word prick.

The visitors she has overlap at times, to my sister's annoyance. My father drives himself to the hospital and comes in to the ward after my mother has had a particularly bad day. Seeing other visitors around the bed of another dying woman, he joins in their group, feeling himself to be unwelcome in ours, oblivious to their grave faces and tearful expressions, and shows them his varicose veins, chatting brightly about his ailments. They are not impressed and we have to go after him.

"Dad, these people have come to talk to their relative, they don't want to know about your varicose veins." He looks surprised, turns to us and grins sheepishly like a schoolboy who has just been told off.

"I thought you were talking to your mother, so I would talk to them." He peers at my mother in the bed. She avoids his gaze; can't see him clearly anyway. He goes to her side and takes her hand. She snatches it away — it's the hand with the cannula in and he's hurt her again. He doesn't look, doesn't think. It's hard to remain balanced when he's so thoughtless. He says in a falsely concerned and overloud voice, intended to be heard by others:

"How are you?" Tersely she answers that she is dying. What else can she say? He ignores it.

"Oh, you'll be all right. I'm feeding the dicky birds for you. The robin popped in this morning. He sits there waiting for me to come out and feed him." He chuckles at the memory. She tries to turn her hearing aid up or down, and appears uncomfortable in the bed. There's no indication that she heard him. We lift her up the bed and prop her with pillows. She uses the interruption to address herself to us. My father is cut out of the conversation again.

We hoped she might come home eventually for a spell, but she deteriorated fast for five months until she died. Members of the family came and went. My father had to accept the unacceptable finally, and visited every day, sitting in silence by her bed and, never having learned to communicate with her, was not able to start now. My brother and sister did not generally accompany him on these trips.

The ward was dirty and the nurses too busy to have time for individual treatment of their patients. Chicken bones dropped by my mother from a previous meal because she couldn't see where to put them were left under her chair for days and her hearing aid, her life line, was often left switched off. I was made angry by the treatment of the old and terminally ill in our hospitals, who do not need medication as much as love and attention and reassurance while they get on with the business of dying.

And all the while she was dying, it was a perfect Indian summer, warm and fine, and the mushrooms along the verges and in the suburban gardens gave a dazzling display; fruiting bodies, decaying slowly, feeding on rottenness. I struggled to find a message there. Life comes out of decay and death, I thought. My mother's death might yet provide a chance for my brother, now middle aged, to free himself and begin to live, my sister to find another person to attach to, to find love somewhere else.

As she drew closer to her own death my mother told her grandchildren, our sons, that she expected them to wear dark suits to her funeral.

"I say, Caroline, " she whispered hoarsely, "You will tell your people to wear suits to the funeral, won't you?"

"Of course. We promise, don't we?" And they all promised, and kept their promises. They were fond of their grandmother and in her last days talked to her with affection and respect. She talked about the coming event freely and said she wondered how my brother would manage after her death. He must have wondered the same.

TWENTY-TWO

My mother wants to give our second son the gift she will leave him in her will. It is a set of ivory chess pieces, very old and ornate. We find them and take them to the hospital where she gives them to him, watched by the envious eyes of Janet, who does not want him to have them. Our youngest son has a carved wooden bear; very Victorian, which he has always admired and been afraid of simultaneously. Again my sister struggles with this. There is nothing for our foster son, despite his devotion and willingness to run errands and help in any way he can. In my mother's eyes, he isn't family and as such could never be included. This ability to hurt others by omitting them from things is what has driven our family for generations.

The will, when it is read, leaves a small legacy of two thousand pounds to my father. That's all. The rest of her money is divided between my sister and me, and the house goes to my brother. My father is very bitter and rips the cheque up. There is no crumb of comfort for him anywhere.

The gift she has left her oldest grandson is her books. I am pleased for him, and he is pleased when I tell him on the phone in New Zealand where he has just started a new job. I am shocked to hear my sister say that she has the Felix journals and thinks they should stay in the family. She means by this that they should stay with her. We are deeply hurt by this. We search for the little book of simples. It is nowhere to be found. I am disgusted. I look for other books that might have some meaning or value to Rob and find that they are all missing.

I ask the solicitor for advice and she is shocked. I write a letter to my sister, asking for the books back, but she refuses.

Months later, as we have to meet again for the probate forms to be signed, I stay for the last time at Somersets. Janet and I are supposed to divide up the jewellery and our mother's other things. I consider this. I have always given her things—nice presents, books and fabrics, jewellery and interest and encouragement, which I think she values. I realise later how I have been duped by those big tearful eyes. We divide up my mother's jewellery and I give it all, except the items specifically left to me, to my sister. Clearly she needs so much, but nothing will ever be enough, and I know I have a life she will never have; her attachment to my mother was too anxious and troubled to allow her to attach to anyone else. I understand how bereft she feels; my mother took the place of husband, baby, cherished pet, and now she's gone. In vain I talk to my sister over the phone, hoping she'll relent and give back some of what she's taken, or suggest a compromise. Could she make copies of the Felix books and let Rob have those? She slams the phone down on me. I ask my brother if I can look through the books in what is now his house to see if I can find the book of simples, but he is too full of irrational anger with my mother for leaving him and directs that anger full force at me, my husband, the neighbours and the outside world. He has no one left in the world now that he cares about, except for Janet, and he's scared of her. She wants to own the house, move in and take over. He isn't sure he wants that, but she's bigger than he is and he's scared of her; scared of her big tearful eyes and fierce temper. His life has been run by a woman who never allowed him his own life. Why would he want to let that happen again? My sister says then that my mother said she could keep the books just before she died. So they stay with her. Janet cannot bear to think that my mother would have shared her love with her grandsons. I feel deeply hurt by this. Things don't take the place of people I remind myself, but her selfishness and dishonesty are hard to stomach when my own children are denied what their grandmother left them. I can't like her anymore, and I cease pretending to.

TWENTY-THREE

Janet is holding forth after my mother's death.

"She didn't want a religious funeral. She hated the church." My father doesn't believe it.

"She said so?"

"Oh yes. Many times." There is no discussion. It is said with a sneer at my father. Okay, I think, we can arrange something else. My father is not happy.

The humanist lady wants to meet the family to discuss the arrangements. It is assumed by my brother and sister that my father will not join us. He wants his wife to have a Christian burial. But the humanist lady makes a point of inviting him, and he is grateful for this. So am I. We decide on Wordsworth and a poem suggested by the humanist lady. My father wants 'The Last Rose of Summer" to be played. My sister sniffs at this. I try to find out some facts about my mother from my father, but he seems to know less about her then we do. I am trying to write the eulogy.

"When did she get her art qualifications, Dad?" He looks at me blankly.

"Did she have some? I don't remember."

"Okay, what can you tell me about her interests and hobbies and things when you met?" But he can remember nothing. Eventually he admits, "You know more about her than I do."

The moment I broke the news to him that she had passed away, he replied that he had better tell his girlfriend the news. I still hadn't quite forgiven him for this. In the kitchen he treated me as he had her, objecting to my cooking and telling me how to do simple things. Explaining that I had had thirty years of practice away from him was a waste of time. Taking down my washing and rehanging it, with a lecture on how washing should be hung led to my explaining, at first gently and then with some force that I was not to be bullied and that I would ask for help if I needed it. When he saw how angry and upset his constant bullying made me, and that I wouldn't stand for it, he stopped for a while and was unhappy until he found other things to bully. I was glad when Steven came to my rescue on the day before the funeral, but his appearance spelled the end of any newfound solidarity with my sister and brother. They froze and withdrew immediately. I asked myself why this was. He had never upset them in any way that I was aware of. Because he had taken me away from the family? Because they had a problem sharing me, or my mother's memory with my partner, even though he had been fond of my mother and she of him? Instead of welcoming in another pair of helping hands, it became clear that my mother's love and the family's inclusion of others was not to be extended to other family members, not even her grandsons and son-in-law.

My sister acted as gatekeeper at the funeral. It was clear that my family was not welcome but had to be allowed to come. Other relations had to be squeezed past her on the grounds of them being insulted if not asked. My sister could not bear to share my mother with anyone, even in death. Only about twelve people came in total, including us. I supported my father throughout the service. He placed a single red rose on the coffin. It looked lonely beside the family bouquet. The humanist had listened to what he wanted and arranged for 'The Last Rose of Summer' to be played as we left the church. My sister sneered at these expressions of sentimentality, but it gave my father comfort. The eulogy, read by the humanist, referred to our parents' first meeting and their long marriage. I watched the hackles on Janet's neck rise with disapproval at this.

The missing legacy continued to cause difficulties, with probate and with my sister. The feelings of my son at being deprived of something representing my mother's love for him were not considered; indeed, he was not even approached about it. On my final stay in the house, I tried to talk to my brother about the missing books, since my sister was so hostile, to ask if I might look for the little book of simples. He refused to speak to me and locked himself in his bedroom. I left the following morning, and it felt very final.

I had a comforting dream about my mother, not long after she died, in which she came down a long corridor to meet me and hugged and kissed me tenderly, saying goodbye. My mother-in-law, herself at the very end of her life, told me that my mother had visited her also and held her hand through the side rails of her bed. Knowing I was about to lose Maggie too was too much to bear, and I couldn't give a sensible response, but I know she derived comfort from the contact. Who am I to argue with things I don't understand? It had been Maggie; always sensible, practical and direct, who had phoned us very early one morning to ask if our middle son was all right. She had a feeling he was in danger. It happened that he was, at that moment, on a small Italian ferry crossing to Brindisi from Pireus and two water spouts had appeared very close to the ship. He had been very frightened by the experience.

It had not been so long ago that my mother and she had met, Maggie coming up the drive to Somersets in her wheelchair, making her way into the house slowly, so slowly, and my mother creeping at her snail's pace towards the door. When they met, it was like an encounter between two ancient tortoises, but my mother clutched Maggie's hand eagerly, recognising a fellow sufferer. Steven and I both wiped tears away. My father looked on, bemused.

The following spring we collected the ashes from the undertaker and Janet stated that they should be placed in the bluebell woods where she took my mother to visit every year.

"She would have wanted her ashes to be sprinkled in the bluebell wood. We used to go there every year; she loved it there." No one else was asked if they felt this was appropriate, or if they had other ideas. We had taken her to the bluebell woods one year and knew how much she enjoyed the experience. The bluebell wood was a long way from the house and my father, although he did not object—how could he? became very tearful on the phone and asked me if I could arrange for some of her ashes to be sprinkled in the country churchyard where they were married. I was not asked for my opinion. I negotiated that we would accompany my father to the churchyard in the morning and arranged this with the priest; then we would take him for lunch as my brother did not offer to play the host, and later go on to the bluebell wood.

The bluebell wood is overgrown and gloomy. Misty violet blue shadows stretch away under the trees. It is a sombre place, and we have driven for about three quarters of an hour to reach it. The path through the trees is uneven, barred with brambles, and dead leaves litter the ground. My father, none too steady on his feet, does not like this at all. He has not walked in a wood for years. Someone has nailed a small artificial bunch of flowers to a tree. It has been there a long time. Another death? Murder, I think, irrationally. Bodies.

My sister strides ahead of us, her face set and stony, the urn clutched under her arm, tightly. My brother follows her. It's as if we weren't there. Janet is almost out of sight, and starts to scatter the ashes. The white flakes fall, coating the brambles and the new leaves. My brother approaches and tries to gesture to her. She stops and lets him take some of the ashes. She does not offer them to us. I go up to her. She is suffering, I tell myself, Mother was all she had. But she has to understand that others have a claim too. My father begins to cry.

He has not had a turn at sprinkling the ashes and he's feeling scared to think of Edith out here, so far away from home, in this creepy wood.

"Douglas, please can you tell Janet that Dad's upset? Can we go back now?" He passes the message on. We are strung out in a line, Steven with my father, holding his arm, me, Douglas and then in front is Janet, throwing ashes bitterly into the brambles and bluebells, not recognising anybody else. Finally she sighs and turns towards us. My father speaks.

"She's so far away from home here. She should be in the garden at Somersets." He weeps again. "I don't like it here. She wouldn't have wanted to be so far away from home." My sister sighs impatiently and releases her grip on the urn just a fraction.

"She's not alone here. Look, someone else has been here." She points to the flowers on the tree. Douglas says nothing. Silently we go back out of the wood and return to the cars and go back to Somersets, where finally my father is allowed, grudgingly, to sprinkle some ashes. My sister holds the almost empty urn out to me, as if reluctantly offering me a sweet. She does not let go of it, does not look at me. It is impossible for her to let go, even for a moment. My father is slightly happier. We go into the house, and as Douglas does not offer to make a drink, I make one before Steven and I leave this house and its occupants behind to go back to our own lives. I have never before experienced such bitterness, such hatred, such disregard for the feelings of others, even knowing as I do the madness that grief can bring. How will my father survive in this house, with Douglas not speaking to him and Janet so indifferent to his feelings? Whatever he deserves, surely we can rise above this and offer him something? I visit when I can and spend hours on the phone, talking to him.

I hope he may decide he doesn't want to live in this house that isn't his with a depressed, non-communicative son. But he's frightened to move and resorts to killing squirrels to get rid of his anger. I think to myself that my father has been rejected all his life, and my mother's final rejection of him in her will has made it clear that he is unwelcome anywhere. I urge my brother to tell me if he gets ill, or if I can help in any way.

Later, my father slips on the wood floor and cuts his head open, needing twenty stitches. I find out about this only when I ring my father and ask to speak to him, several days after this happens. It's the same when he has a hip replaced. My brother lets it be known that I am not welcome in his house, neither is Steve, who he accuses of leaning on him to sell the house. As this is patently nonsense, I ignore it. Douglas does not want to sell the house; anyway, Janet wouldn't let him. It makes no difference to me financially, whether it's sold or not, but on balance, I would prefer Douglas to have the chance of a life outside this place and if selling it would give him that option, then good luck to him, I think.

TWENTY-FOUR

My father, the engineer, is sitting beside me now. His freckled bald head is shining in the sunlight as he sits in the garden of my brother's house, drinking tea, the wisps of white hair that remain are lightly fluffed in the breeze. His big nose and blue eyes, now beginning to be dim, give his a face a distinction in old age that in youth he did not possess. A slight smile is on his lips, as he muses on the way he told musicians at the folk club about Wheatcroft and the making of concertinas. While we are with him, he has an audience of people who understand his need for attention and will listen to his reminiscences, until growing restless, they wander away and find that he hasn't noticed they've gone. But what does he have when we're not there? An empty house with only my brother around in the evenings, shut in his own little room, while my father spreads his papers and rubbish over the downstairs rooms and takes over all the living space. My brother is not able to say that it's his house now, and he wants to live in more of it; wants to own it properly. He would have to confront my father to do this and that he is unable to do. True, he feels (and says) that my father would not cope with the change, and maybe he's right, and he feels some guilt that he has a house and my father is only a lodger. But there's another side too — he needs my father's money, what there is of it, to maintain the place. My father has paid for a new central heating boiler recently. My brother would not have been able to pay for it himself, what with the inheritance tax he has to find. But he dislikes being beholden to my father. My father would be glad in many ways to be away from there, but in a world that has always treated him with exasperation and dislike, where will he find a safe haven?

I feel sure I could offer him something more than he has now, though how I can manage that from a practical point of view remains to be seen.

His cruel streak is not in evidence now. In the years after my mother died and he could not bully anyone, he turned his attentions to the creatures in the garden, first the squirrels and then the magpies. The squirrels he caught in wire traps, and drowned slowly in the water butt, enjoying watching them suffer. The magpies he tried to shoot with my brother's airgun. My brother stopped him, unwilling to see small creatures suffer unnecessarily. So he had to learn to contain his feelings of rage and wanting to kill things and found as he did so others came closer to him and were able to join him in his isolation. The phone calls between us were many, as I tried to explain to him the effect of his behaviour and tell him, as he couldn't grasp it for himself, how other people were feeling and the reasons for their behaviour. He did listen, but needed to be reminded again and again that my brother was an adult, capable of making his own decisions and would not want to be told what to do all the time. He couldn't understand this at all.

"But if I know the best way to do something, surely I should tell him?"

"Does he listen if you do?"

Silence. Finally he answers. "No. Doesn't listen to anybody. Should do."

"So telling him is no use?"

"Probably not."

"Well, Dad, people usually prefer to ask for help or advice if they need it, rather than having it imposed on them. I mean, you're like that too, aren't you? You don't like being told what to do." He ponders this a while.

"I see what you mean. But if it's in his interests to listen and learn something ..."

"Then he'll ask."

He changes the subject at this point. I will have to say this again, many times. To him, my brother is a child still, who knows nothing and is incapable of leading his own life. Unfortunately my brother believes this too, and is far more helpless than he needs to be, paralysed by years of living with my parents.

I haven't spoken to my brother or my sister in any meaningful way for several years now. I decided it wasn't worth it. Every time I went near them, the anger they carried would surface and I would leave feeling stupid that I had let it happen again. I was not willing to be their punchbag; the anger they felt was not with me, but with our parents and themselves, for not becoming the adult people they could have been.

My father will never change; he is now as he always has been, a man only concerned with his own status and survival, but something has changed. Dimly he realises that other people are separate living, breathing creatures, capable of being hurt. What he has learned is that his survival depends on those around him being content, and that expressing an interest in their welfare, even if it's only a cursory enquiry, is likely to make others warm to him more. He has lived in his isolated little world for so long that he is danger of forgetting who he is, and goes over the same life story again and again. My mother's deafness also locked her into isolation, but she was more able to respond to the needs of others, in fact, would worry about them, reminding me when we met of families she had encountered when staying with us and their problems, when they had long moved on.

The phone calls from him become madder. He rings often. Sometimes there is a note of triumph.

"Dad here. You know, I've found the cause of the problem. Grapefruit."

"Grapefruit?"

"Yes. Grapefruit have some poison in them that attacks the nerve endings. That stabbing pain I had in my side, they x-rayed it, you know, but they couldn't find a thing. Grapefruit, that's what it is." I'm lost for words. Finally I respond.

"So if you don't eat grapefruit, your aches and pains will go away?"

"Damn sure of it. Before the war, they started growing grapefruit and they were supposed to take out the poison, but they didn't. My physiotherapist agrees with me." So that's that. I bet the physio didn't say anything of the sort, I think.

"So you're going to leave out grapefruit and see if it makes a difference?"

"Pity, because I like it."

Well, what harm can it do? It's another straw for him to clutch at.

I have just come out of hospital myself, following a cancer scare, and he knows this. He does not ask about this, however, as usual he has blanked it out as of little relevance to him. When I tell him my stay in hospital went well and that I'll have the results of the tests later, he does not respond. He has to know that I am a person too, that I share some anxieties about my own health. I want him to express concern, and when I push it under his nose, he does pause for a moment to consider what it might mean. His own health, quite good considering his age, is the only concern he has. He finds new aches and pains to tell me about, each time appearing puzzled by his increasing frailty.

The fact that he is in his late eighties and has had one hip replaced, followed by a serious wound infection does not enter his calculations. Everything is repairable, if you know what's wrong with it. He is an engineer; anything that can't be explained must be magic.

My father feels now that his current bad health has been inflicted on him by Aunt Ethel, who has cursed him from the grave. He is losing his memory and thinks that the names, dates and objects he mislays have been hidden from him, or have somehow moved themselves without his knowledge. Magical thinking has always formed a part of his personality, and logic and reason play no part. He wants the house to be exorcised.

The problem with the evil squirrels was that they might get into the house and cause chaos, so they had to be killed. These fiends from out there might enter his domain and wreak destructive havoc. He could not allow them to intrude. Basil Hamborough, his stepfather, had wanted him dead, many years ago, when he was a child. He had seen an evil face at the window at his prep school and realised it was Basil, looking for him. As my father was on the first floor of the school block, this was more likely to have been a vivid dream than a reality. Such incidents are commonplace for him; the dividing line between reality, dreams and fantasy is very blurred. He claimed that Basil sent parcels to him at the school containing sweets, but in each parcel were also things that would harm him—scorpions, spiders. He remembers Basil creeping into his bedroom, intent on suffocating him with a pillow. Whatever the truth of it, he was certainly moved around in the school holidays from relative to relative, in a bid to keep one step ahead of Basil, and his father told him later they feared his life had been in danger. He was not allowed to see his mother until Basil had left the marriage, realising at last that killing my father would not enable him to get his hands on Bill's money, which was tied up in a trust fund that not even she could touch.

His mother hadn't wanted him, his much loved nurse maid left the family, his stepmother had him sent away to boarding school at seven, his girlfriend decided to marry someone else, his wife sided with the children against him and now he knows that two of those children want him dead and gone from their lives. How much is of his making currently, he doesn't, will never, grasp now.

The little book of simples has appeared, suddenly, in the drawer where it should have been all along, but this isn't magic, it's a guilty conscience at work. I'm glad to have it anyway, though as Rob's not around to receive it, I have to tell him I now have it safe. He's pleased, but the rift with Janet will never be healed, not now.

One Monday morning there's a phone call from my father.

"Dad here. Just thought I should let you know. I woke up yesterday and I couldn't see out of my left eye. Went over to the hospital and they say it's a blocked artery. There's no hope. He tried to unblock it, but he says the sight won't come back. Got to go and see him again on Thursday. They're worried about the other eye. Just thought you should know." I am horrified. There's been no word from my brother or sister, and he's alone in the house, half blind, unsure whether he will lose the sight in his other eye.

He seems quite sanguine about it. Attention is what he craves and he has a legitimate means of obtaining it now. This will involve more hospital visits and sympathy from others. Before, it was his legs, ulcerated and weeping that had needed weekly dressing and ensured he received regular physical attention and care. His nurses told me that as soon as they healed his legs, he would sabotage their efforts, and that they recognised this as his need for company and attention. They accepted this fact and made allowances by making him the last of their home visits, so that his need to talk would not make them late for their next patient. They gave up their lunch hours for him and it never occurred to him that their visits to him were anything less than enjoyable.

His loss of sight in one eye gives him a great deal of temporary mileage in terms of attention and sympathy. But he becomes bored with it. He decides the grapefruit are to blame for his blindness, as for all his ills (when it isn't a curse put on him by Ethel) and that his sight is returning a little now he no longer eats them. I express hope with him, without colluding in this extraordinary belief.

His conversations with me become more limited and confined to his own bodily functions. I assume that his nurses too have had to endure detailed descriptions of his constipation, wind and leaking bladder. Although I stop him at a point where I feel nauseated and tell him I don't want to hear details of his intimate functions, he pays little attention. His nurses may not have felt so bold. He has nothing else to talk about, except the past, and even he is getting bored with that.

His decision to leave Somersets was hard for him, as well as for us. For months he had phoned me and two other people concerned with his welfare, to say how miserable he was and how he longed for extra support and help and company. My brother did the best he could, but his work commitments and poor health as well as his reluctance to engage with my father's rambling monologues, meant that my father was essentially on his own. He did not want to live at Somersets any more but felt in the meantime that a holiday away from the place might help. His weekly nurse agreed and gave him every encouragement and accordingly we made plans to offer him a short respite with us, with an opportunity to look at some residential places in the area. He was happy with this idea, so we hired a wheelchair and planned the trip carefully. True to form, when we went to fetch him, he had changed his mind. Not even the promise of an evening at the local folk club where he could play his concertina swayed him, though it was a near thing. He changed his mind again several times in the course of our visit, finally pronouncing himself unable to get into the car, and finally we had to decide to take him to the pub in the wheelchair for lunch and call it a day. He wore his panama hat as the day was hot, and we paraded slowly through the village with the wheelchair to the pub, where he drank cider and ate a bacon and salad sandwich, followed by ice-cream. He had not been feeding himself at home very well, and was hungry. My previous attempts to arrange for him to visit a luncheon club failed when he was rude to the organiser and changed his mind about trying this out. As always, he knew just how to cause maximum inconvenience. He had not been out of the house for six months, except to the hospital.

We had a wager that he would change his mind about the holiday at the last minute; it's very typical of narcissistic people, so we weren't too thrown by his change of mind. Once again I felt as though I was drawn towards him in an effort to assist at his request, only to be slapped hard the minute I was close enough. My brother and sister, not realising how pervasive this pattern is, have followed suit. Yet his sadness and sense of isolation and rejection are very real; only this knowledge has prevented me hating him. He is giving back what the world gave him all those years ago and he cannot stop himself.

In his lucid moments he talks to me as if I were a real person:

"I did love your mother, you know, Caroline."

"I know you did, Dad. In your own way."

"I wanted her to come to Bournmouth with me, you know, when I went to the concertina convention, but I could never persuade her to come."

"That's because she always wanted to go to Scotland. I'm just glad I was able to arrange that for her before she died."

"I don't know why she wanted to go to Scotland. She could have had a good time in Bournmouth."

"But the point is that she wanted to go to Scotland. It wasn't your choice; your choice was Bournmouth, but it was her choice. She resented never having her choice."

"I see what you mean. But Bournmouth would have been much better." I begin to tire.

"Dad, you and Mum should have sorted this stuff out between you. As you know, I've never taken sides with you and Mum. I cared for you both and it made me very sad that you couldn't get on better than you did. I wanted you both to be happy and it's been difficult being stuck in the middle, being expected to take sides." He's silent now, unusually for him. Something I said must have hit home.

"You've been a good daughter Caroline, and I love you." Do my ears deceive me? No, Stephen heard it too. For once, he meant it. I swallow tears.

Later:

"You know, Caroline, you'd have enjoyed that tape I made of the

Viennese Opera Company. Beautiful stuff. Did I ever send you the tape?"

"No, Dad, I don't think you did."

"Pity." He shakes his head sadly. There's a pause. "Your mother missed so much, being deaf. She would have enjoyed it, but she wouldn't listen to it. I did try, Caroline, to make her happy."

"I know, Dad, I know. Things don't always turn out the way you want them to."

It was a stroke, a major one this time; that finally took him away from Somersets. He had been lying on the floor for some time before Douglas found him and the ambulance had problems getting up the drive because of the overhanging branches. For months he lay in the hospital bed, trying to regain the ability to swallow, walk or move his left arm. He lay, unmoving, his eyes shut, for most of this time. Visiting, I held his hand and called his name.

"Dad? It's Caroline." The old milky blue grey eyes opened with an effort, and his face registered some pleased recognition.

"Caroline?"

"Yes, Dad, I'm here."

"I was dreaming about being in Jimmy's Bar."

"Where you used to go with your mother, in the South of France?"

"Jimmy was her boyfriend then."

"What was your dream?"

"Nothing. I was just there at night, watching."

"And did you tango there? Was there dancing?"

"Oh yes, they danced beautifully."

"And did you dance?"

"No, I could rumba, but the tango was too difficult."

"Was it a large place, then, with a dance floor?"

"They danced outside, in the courtyard. Jimmy could dance. There was a band." It's an effort for him, remembering, even more of an effort talking. A nurse comes across, unused to hearing my father talk at all. The stroke has exhausted him.

"Dad is quite an expert on Latin American music, especially the tango," I tell her. She raises her eyebrows. "He has a wonderful collection of records, all early stuff, and quite a lot of it has been borrowed and re-mastered and issued as CDs, and he's written the sleeve notes." I tail off. She's not interested. He's just a bed blocker in her eyes; one of those who cannot really recover enough to go home and who inconveniently refuses to die. Fortunately, his consultant is more understanding. I tell her a little about him, as he is unable to.

"We often don't know what sort of people our patients are, or what their lives have been about," she says. "It helps to know something about them; they're not just bodies in beds, after all." I am grateful for her acknowledgement.

Dad is sleeping again. Later, Douglas and Janet will come to see him. They will stand there, awkwardly, unused to talking to him, listening to him, being with him. Our mother never chose to do this, unless her children were not there. How can they start to pay attention to him now, when he has never really acknowledged them as people? There is no love there, little real pity. They will not touch his hand, they would find that repulsive. He has never received affection in this family and they won't start now, even when he's dying. It's agony for them, this business. They will call his name instead and hope he doesn't respond. If he does, they will not know how to respond, neither will he. After five minutes they will give up, feeling they have done their duty.

I have something to return to, some balance to my life they cannot have. I fear for them, once he's gone.

He lies in a limbo land of slumber from which few people can rouse him. I am his daughter and I understand him somewhat. There's no one else around who is available, they're all dead, or too frail to travel. It's lonely out here, being the engineer's daughter. When he dies, I will try to tell Douglas and Janet that we have all lost him, whatever he meant to us, and that whatever their relationship (on non-relationship) with him, his passing needs to be acknowledged properly. We owe him that, at least.

Somersets is empty of everyone except my brother now. The dark branches of the trees that line the driveway catch at the clothing of any visitors that come to call. It could be the setting for a horror movie, so neglected has it become. The paint is flaking off the window-sills, the gutters sag as if despondent and need only a few more soggy leaves in order to collapse under the weight and give up the ghost. A fox has made her home under the acacia tree, and despite that rabbits roam freely on the lawn, now uncut since my father is not there to oversee it. The porch where Great-Aunt Ethel sat on her daybed on sunny days with her African grey parrot for company is full of my sister's plants and the windows are stained with green algae. No one has been in there for months. The patio my father built around the house from substandard bricks, destroying my sister's herb garden and finally forcing her to leave, is cracked and untidy now, as each frost or summer day flakes off more brick and leaves more hiding places for the ants that are everywhere. The rose arch my father erected has fallen down and has not been replaced, and the shed, still full of plumbing parts and mouse-eaten barrels of fabric saved by my sister, is eerily full of leaves that have blown in. Grime obscures the windows.

The jolly woman who came in to clean and befriend my father has ceased to work here, and inside the place looks unkempt and scruffy without her to maintain a semblance of order. The whole place shows the neglect and disappointment of its inhabitants, and it's worse now, much worse. Douglas is paralysed by the enormity of the task he faces. He has no energy or will to tackle any of it. He has no escape hatch, except that he could sell the house and move away, but will probably be unable to. If he manages it, he'll probably spend a long time travelling, learning that the world is as good as we make it. There is goodness and friendship in the world, despite what my mother believed, or half believed, and the practical skills he inherited from our father may be a useful legacy after all.

The tools my father used, for making musical instruments, for repairing and restoring our furniture, for fixing boilers and carving wood, for gluing joints and soldering metal, are still on the bench where he left them. The shelves above hold tins and jars of screws, nuts, bolts, joints, rivets, washers, pins, staples, nails, jig saw blades, files, chains, screwdrivers and scraps of brass wire, aluminium sheeting, veneer and all the glues, sizes and fluxes that accompany them. He won't see them again.

Before his last stroke, he discovered that the small plastic component in the toilet cistern upstairs was broken. Unable to drive after his hip replacement at eighty-four and unwilling to ask Douglas to buy a new replacement part, he sat up very late at this work bench making a replacement component out of wood, muttering all the while about the shoddiness of today's workmanship and the throw away culture he despises. The component works still, a testimony to his doggedness and practical skill.

His music collection, which is large, and his address books, scrapbooks and tools will all have to be sorted out one day. This is his legacy.

None of the men in my life has real practical ability; they are good with people, artistic and fun to be with, but they can't fix things the way he did. I have some practical skills, can work with small fiddly pieces to assemble something, love the challenge of flat pack furniture, am not put off by instructions, manuals or tools. But mainly my tinkering has been with people and their families, a different sort of engineering if you like, but one I recognise as valid.

I put on a CD he gave me. It's a mix of some of the original Cuban tracks remastered from his records, recordings of one of his early favourites, Dom Barreto, and it's fabulous music. At my feet is a large plastic tub, full of tapes he made me, some featuring himself singing and playing the concertina, some featuring his friends, some copies he's taken of his records.

I haven't begun to listen to them all yet, and I shall take my time, because they tell me more about him than anything else I have, and when he's no longer here, I shall remember that he gave me what he had, which wasn't what I wanted or needed when I was young, but it was all he had to give. And I do treasure it.